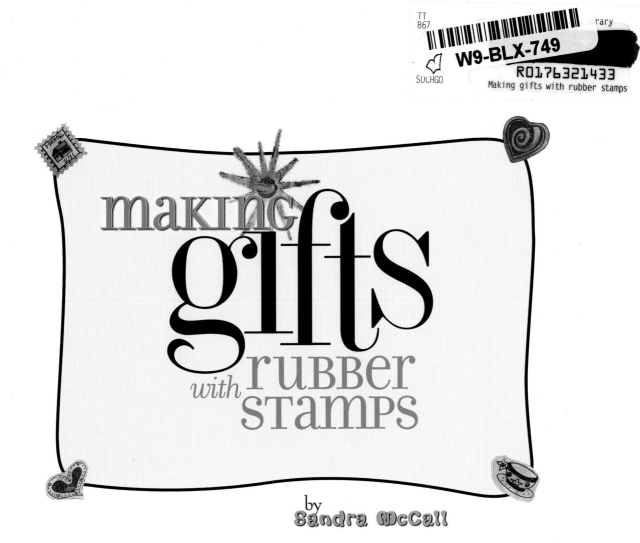

making gifts with rubber stamps

by **Sandra McCall**

NORTH LIGHT BOOKS

CINCINNATI, OHIO

www.nlbooks.com

ABOUT *the* AUTHOR

SANDRA MCCALL comes to this project book by way of an extensive art background that has driven her into the arena of art stamping and collage. A freelance artist living in Southern California with her husband, Les Gains, and their cat, Buddy, Sandra enjoys finding new ways to marry basic art supplies and stamp-related products. Her primary interests include bookbinding, surface embellishment on both paper and fabric, collage and multi-media assemblage.

Sandra has written several successful how-to articles for *Somerset Studios*, *National Stampagraphic* and *The Rubber Stamper*. Her work has also been included in *Rubberstampmadness* and *The Studio*. *Rubberstampmadness* profiled her and her work techniques in the October 1999 issue. Sandra has made guest appearances on HGTV's *Carol Duvall Show*.

Making Gifts With Rubber Stamps. © 2000 by Sandra McCall. Manufactured in China. All rights reserved. The patterns in this book are for the personal use of the reader. By permission of the author and publisher, they may be either hand-traced or photocopied to make single copies, but under no circumstances may they be resold or republished. It is permissible for the purchaser to use the designs herein and sell them at fairs, bazaars and craft shows. No other part of the book may be reproduced in any form or by any electronic or mechanical means including information storage and retrieval systems without permission in writing from the publisher, except by a reviewer, who may quote brief passages in a review. Published by North Light Books, an imprint of F&W Publications, Inc., 1507 Dana Avenue, Cincinnati, Ohio 45207, (800) 289-0963. First edition.

05 04 03 02 01 5 4 3 2

Library of Congress Cataloging-in-Publication Data
McCall, Sandra.
    Making gifts with rubber stamps / by Sandra McCall.
      p. cm.
    Includes index.
    ISBN 1-58180-081-9
    1. Rubber stamp printing. 2. Gifts. I. Title.

TT867 .M345 2000
761—dc21
              00-033258

Editor: Jane Friedman
Designer: Stephanie Strang
Production artist: Donna Cozatchy
Production coordinator: Emily Gross
Photographers: Christine Polomsky and Al Parrish

Sandra teaches paper arts classes in stores and at conventions across the country. Her classes provide a relaxed atmosphere where students can benefit from the sharing of information and skills. She says that she is happy if she is successful in teaching her students to have no fear and to try everything artwise. She sums up her view of the artist in this way: You may call yourself an "artist" when you are mature enough to realize two things. First, you will never stop learning because you realize that you will never know everything about anything, and second, you create because you *have* to.

acknowledgments

Without the constant source of information and inspiration that comes from my real family and my other family, my students, this book wouldn't have been possible. Thanks also to my wonderful editor, Jane Friedman, and my talented photographer, Christine Polomsky.

✳

dedication

FOR MY MOM,
Betty Jean Cox Griffiths, the best cheerleader any girl could have. Irish, this one's for you.

Table of Contents

MIXED MEDIA

a useful introduction

"RUBBER STAMP ART. ISN'T THAT AN OXYMORON?" you ask. Trust me, I've heard that far too often—and it's time to put an end to that ridiculous and prejudiced belief. The image on the stamp may have been drawn by somebody else, but a stamp is really another great accessory to add to your collection of art tools. Just as a hammer has been forged by someone else, so have your rubber stamps—and so what? Use your rubber stamps as tools to create something fabulous and uniquely your own. Do not pay attention to the limitations set by some unenlightened soul on this matter: True artists will take a rubber stamp and use it to add yet another very cool and textural dimension to their work. They will see not just an image drawn by another, but an image that is begging to be taken a step further into another realm of creativity. Your creativity! The techniques used to texture the projects in this book are easily translated to cardmaking, so think about the possibilities as you read through each project. All of the projects in this book have lots of options, so think openly and creatively, substitute supplies and techniques and have a blast with them!

Now, I was instructed to write an introduction, but I can't stand reading intros about how I had this great idea for a book and how it all came about and blah, blah, blah… So, here's a page with some useful information. The following pointers are things that were not mentioned in the step-by-steps because there just didn't seem to be a good place to put them. I think you'll agree, though, that they are pointers worth knowing.

Project dimensions *

All of my students will tell you that I hate, hate, HATE listing dimensions of projects because I think you need to think about it and understand how you can make any project the size that you need. For my class descriptions, I try to explain how the cover of a handmade book has to be about ¼" (6mm) larger than the text block, whatever that size may be. To make you feel more secure, I'll list measurements in this book, but remember: Only pay attention to how much larger or smaller each piece needs to be and then substitute your own measurements for the overall size that is suited to your needs.

Chipboard *

You can find chipboard in various weights from lots of sources—the back sides of writing tablets, cereal boxes and on and on. In a pinch, it is perfectly OK to glue two sheets of chipboard together to get a thicker board for your projects. Try to use chipboard or book board for your book projects. Mat board is a plied material and will separate more readily than chipboard. Do try to avoid using foamcore for books because it dents and bends. I only mention it because I've seen

book covers made from foamcore, and it is a shame to put a lot of work into your book only to get dents in it the first time you drop it.

Plastic sheets *

Several of the projects in this book call for plastic sheets. Look in your phone book for a plastic store near you. Almost every town has one. Acrylic, styrene and Plexiglas all fall under the general heading of "plastics." If you buy Plexiglas or acrylic, you will need to buy a plastic cutter. It's used just like a glass cutter to gouge out a channel. Then snap the plastic for a clean break. Scissors will probably crack the acrylic or Plexiglas. I prefer to use thin styrene in class because it can be cut and trimmed with long-bladed tin snips or an old pair of heavy-duty scissors. To make the holes, I use a little Fiskars hand drill or a pin vise.

OK, I think that's it.
GO FORTH AND MAKE ART!

BASIC SUPPLIES

IN RUBBER STAMP ART, YOU WILL UN-DOUBTEDLY USE A VARIETY OF ART MA-TERIALS. LET'S GO OVER THE MATERIALS USED IN THE PROJECTS IN THIS BOOK.

Stamps *

Generally, the deeper the etching on a rubber stamp, the better quality the stamp. A deeper image will allow better depth for stamping on clay, a better impression for stamping on fabric, and will stand up to more abuse.

You can purchase unmounted stamps (just the rubber image, with no wood or cushion) through the mail, at conventions or at some rubber stamp stores. They can be stored in three-ring binders in pocket holders or in sheet protectors. There are a variety of mounting methods for unmounted stamps. I often use double-stick tape between a block of acrylic and the unmounted stamp, as you'll see pictured in some photos. If a large, unmounted stamp will not stamp clearly, you can add a cushion by attaching a layer of fun foam to the back of the unmounted stamp with rubber cement.

Stamp selection

Choose different stamps for different projects. For instance, you will want a bold image and a deeply etched stamp rather than a very detailed image for stamping in clay or for doing monoprints.

Heat gun *

My favorite heat gun is the Milwaukee. It melts embossing powder fast and it's inexpensive. It does have a strong airstream though, so you may want to get one of the smaller guns with a lower temp and slower airstream. The smaller guns work well to shrink plastic and emboss items into your powder, such as glitter stars and other light things you don't want to blow off the table.

Paintbrushes *

An inexpensive, disposable brush with a feathered tip is a great tool for texturing cards with paint, ink and bleach. A large, very soft camel-hair paintbrush is good for brushing off excess embossing powder. Foam brushes are good for smoothing on paste for paste paper or for applying aged-metal products such as rust and green patinas. You'll want to designate a brush for applying Perfect Paper Adhesive for decoupage. You should also have a variety of brushes for watercolors and other paints.

Brayer

A brayer is used for many purposes. I use mine to smooth large, glued surfaces, to brayer rainbow ink onto cardstock, to ink a monoprinting plate, to ink stamps with viscous permanent ink and to ink my wood and lino cuts. There are several types of brayers on the market, including soft foam and those with decorative rollers attached, but you will want to start with one soft rubber brayer for general purposes. Protect your rollers: They can be marred. Remember to set and store your brayer roller side up if you have a soft brayer.

Portable paper cutter

I love this cutter because it fits perfectly on the little shelf at my right-hand side so I can grab it and cut in a jiff without having to get up from the worktable. For more perfect cuts you will want another cutter, but for quick and small jobs this one is excellent.

Awl

You'll use this for punching holes into items such as chipboard, leather or a stack of papers to be stab bound.

Pin vise

This is available at hobby shops. It is a handle with different-size chucks to hold a variety of small drill bits. You can easily drill through anything simply by turning the pin vise like a screwdriver. I use it on chipboard, polymer clay and paperclay, and to drill out beads that need a bigger hole.

Needle-nose tweezers

This is for placement of small items such as beads and even for picking up small papers in decoupage or collage.

Scissors

Buy three pairs and label one for paper, one for fabric and one for metal and chipboard. Use each pair for those items exclusively. Paper, metal and chipboard will dull your fabric scissors. Also, chipboard will dull and torque the blades, making the tips close unevenly. You'll also want a pair of small scissors for cutting fine details into paper.

Paper punches

You'll need two paper punches, one ¼" (6mm) and another ⅛" (3mm). These are used for making holes for charms of lightweight chipboard and in shrink plastic before they're heated. They are also useful for punching clean holes for eyelets.

Pliers

You want small round-nose pliers with a niche for cutting wire for use in handling jump rings and wire.

Utility knife

This cuts chipboard or mat board.

Craft knife

This is for cutting papers and for scoring chipboard.

Stylus

A couple different sizes will be handy for dry embossing on paper and scoring paper and chipboard. I also use it to mark soft clay.

Straightedge

Buy a good metal ruler in a length that will accommodate most of your projects. A useful size for me is 15" (42 cm). The cork backing will keep the ruler from slipping over your work. It also raises the metal surface off the paper so that if you use a marker along it, the ink will not bleed under the ruler, making a marred line.

Cutting mat

Get a good quality mat that is self healing and has grid marks that are easy to read. Note: Do not use your heat gun on your cutting mat.

hints

Heat gun When you have to emboss something small or you are shrinking a piece of plastic, you may want to set the item into a small, shallow box to keep it from flying off the table. It's also helpful to start the heat gun right over the object to capture it in the airflow. Starting the gun and then moving it onto the object will push it out of position.

Computer mouse pad For the stamps that need cushion under the paper (in order to stamp a clear image), I use a computer mouse pad

Repairing rubber stamps If, in all your cleaning and general abuse, the rubber separates from the cushion, use rubber cement to glue it back together.

CHIPBOARD *and* PAPER

ONE OF THE MOST COMMONLY USED
PRODUCTS IN BOOKBINDING AND THE
CONSTRUCTION OF PAPER BOXES IS
CHIPBOARD. CHIPBOARD (NOT TO BE
CONFUSED WITH CARDBOARD) COMES IN
A VARIETY OF THICKNESSES AND IS
FOUND AT MOST ART SUPPLY STORES.

THE PAPERS USED IN THESE PROJECTS
ARE GENERALLY CLASSIFIED AS TEXT,
CARDSTOCK OR HANDMADE; ALL CAN BE
FOUND IN MOST ART SUPPLY STORES.

Chipboard *

Chipboard is an inexpensive, multipurpose material—the same stuff used for cereal boxes and the back of paper tablets. For all projects in the book, I've used caliper sizes 0.050 and 0.100.

Most art supply stores carry chipboard that has an acid-free white paper coating on both sides. It's called Davey Board and is quite a bit more expensive than regular chipboard.

Text-weight paper *

Text-weight paper is lighter and is used for the text blocks (interior pages) of books or for wrapping chipboard covers and boxes.

- *bond* — generally a lightweight, 20lb smooth-surfaced typing or copy paper great for stamping and monoprinting.
- *kraft* — usually tan, easily glued paper that commonly ranges from about 20lb to 80lb.
- *white, recycled sketch paper* — 50lb is a good weight to work with; it's easily manipulated and glued.

Cardstock *

Cardstock is a general term for stiffer, heavier paper used for cards and small gift box construction.

- *white index* — the one I buy is an inexpensive 110lb found in most office supply stores.
- a variety of colored stock in the 110lb to 150lb range.

Handmade papers *

You may choose handmade papers to adorn some projects in this book. Here are some suggestions.

- Japanese lace paper — try it with collage or on boxes.
- 90lb Arches cold-pressed watercolor paper — I used it with the lampshades.
- Joss paper — a thin, beige Asian paper that has a rectangle of applied silver leafing in the center, also good for collage and boxes.
- Canson Mi-Tientes drawing paper (75lb) — try it out on the portfolio pockets and other wrapped projects.

Finding the grain *

All papers, including chipboard, have a long and short grain to them. It is easier to cut on the long grain than against the short grain. When possible, fold a paper on the long grain. Some papers will tend to tear when creased against the short grain. A coated paper is more likely to crack if you fold it against the short grain.

To find the grain of a paper, all you have to do is start to fold it over. If the paper curls inward, toward the fold, you are folding with the long grain. If the paper curls back, away from the direction of the fold, you are folding on the short grain. Scoring your paper before folding it will produce a cleaner, more professional line.

To prepare chipboard for a fold, score the inside of the fold with a stylus and score the outside with your knife. Do not crease a fold past its final angle: For instance, you don't want to flatten a fold that will end with a 90° angle on a box; this will only weaken the chipboard and possibly tear it.

sealants *and* FIXATIVES

THESE ARE THE PRODUCTS THAT I USE
MOST OFTEN. IT'S IMPORTANT TO KNOW
THE DIFFERENCE BETWEEN A SEALANT
AND A FIXATIVE.

Crystal Clear *

This is a quick-drying gloss
coat. It will make the surface
shiny and slick. The surface
will no longer accept watercolor, colored pencil or chalks
with any great success, so
Crystal Clear should be used
as a final coat. Spray light
coats and let dry for a minute
between each coat.

Workable Fixatif *

This is used to add a coat to your
project that will seal the original
work while preparing the surface
to accept more colorants, such as
chalk or colored pencils. Remember to spray light coats. For
instance, if the color of the chalk
darkens, you are applying the
spray too heavily, causing the
chalk to be suspended in the fixative instead
of being secured to the paper as it should be.

Clear Matte *

This is a good, low-odor
sealant when you don't
want a gloss finish, but
again it's a sealant and a
last step, unlike the workable fixatif.

Gloss coat *

These are a few products that I use regularly
for brush-on gloss coats. When I am going to
brush a gloss finish onto a product that used
water-soluble products to color it, I seal the
product with a spray sealant first. This keeps
the colors from running when the coating is
brushed onto the project.

Diamond Glaze. (also Dimensional Magic
and 3-D Crystal Lacquer) These are water-
soluble when wet and are easy to apply. Just
squeeze a little onto the surface to be coated,
and move it around evenly with the tip of the
applicator or a paintbrush. You can make
your own colors with these products by mixing one tiny drop of dye re-inker to about a
half teaspoon of lacquer. These products are
water cleanup and will give you a nice satin
gloss finish.

Treasure Crystal Cote. This is the only finish that I know of that looks like deep, shiny
resin without the mess of mixing a two-part
product. It dries to the touch in an hour and
takes 24 hours to cure. It is a brush-on product, but you will need a cleaner such as lacquer thinner to clean your brushes.

Clear nail polish. It gives a good, hard, gloss
finish to most surfaces.

INKPADS

THERE ARE SEVERAL DIFFERENT TYPES OF INKPADS AVAILABLE FOR STAMPING THAT YOU SHOULD KNOW ABOUT. THERE ARE WATER-SOLUBLE DYE INKPADS, WATERPROOF DYE INKPADS, PIGMENT INKPADS AND SOLVENT-BASED INKPADS FOR STAMPING ON NONPOROUS SURFACES SUCH AS SHRINK PLASTIC AND METAL.

Dye inkpads *

Dye inkpads come in many colors and are for direct stamping and coloring of paper. They are extremely vivid when stamped on white gloss cardstock, and they dry quickly without embossing.

Pigment inkpads *

Pigment inkpads stay wet longer and are for stamping, embossing and coloring directly onto paper. The ink will not dry well on a gloss cardstock and must be embossed. Matte paper will take pigment very well and has no problem drying if the ink is not too thick. Encore Ultimate Metallic inkpads fall into the pigment ink category.

Waterproof dye inkpads *

The dye inkpads that are waterproof will bead up on plastic and metal, so you will also want to get an ink for nonporous surfaces. These inks are known for their permanence, intense smell and the fact you have to use a solvent-based cleaner to clean the stamps. This ink will dye your stamps—as well as everything else—so do be careful with it. Wear only your craft clothes when you use this ink. The products used for stamping in the home, on tiles for instance, such as ZimInk or Decor it are this type of ink.

Inkpads I use *

Pictured are a few of the inkpads I've used in this book. Starting clockwise at one o'clock is a waterproof inkpad by Printworks. The ink in this pad will not run when you color it with brush markers or watercolors. Almost every company has a waterproof inkpad, so experiment to find one you like best.

The Fabrico inkpad by Tsukineko is for stamping on fabric as well as on clay and wood. This is a pigment inkpad and must be heat set with a heat gun after stamping on wood or fabric. This ink will stay wet for a while, as do all the pigment inkpads, so you may certainly emboss with it.

The little pad is a mini dye ink pad from Clearsnap. The great thing about this size inkpad is that you can better afford all the colors you would never use in a larger size. They are also portable, good for direct-to-paper designs and great for stippling. The middle pad is a large version of the same type of dye inkpad.

The tiny little red inkpad (pigment) is a Little Inker from Hero Arts.

Top Boss is a clear pigment inkpad used for embossing items when you don't want or need any ink color. You would use this to tap clear ink onto surfaces when you want to add a coat of clear embossing powder. It's also useful for coating the rubber stamp so it won't stick when you want an intaglio effect on shrink plastic or hot, thick embossing powder.

The top gold pad is an Encore Ultimate Metallic pad from Tsukineko. It is a pigment inkpad, but you do not have to emboss it if you don't want to. It shows up on dark colors of cardstock a little better than the regular pigment inkpads.

INK

THESE ARE INKS USED TO RE-INK STAMP PADS. I ALSO DOT THEM ONTO A PALLET FOR WATERCOLORING STAMPED IMAGES, FOR ADDING COLOR TO SPONGES AND RE-INKING OR CHANGING THE COLOR IN BRUSH MARKERS, AS WELL AS FOR DIRECT-TO-PAPER DECORATIONS.

Dye re-inkers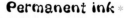

The first two inks pictured are dye re-inkers and are very intense, concentrated color. This makes them great for watercoloring and for use with an airbrush, as well as for re-inking your pads. You'll want to use a tiny drop of color mixed with water for both techniques. This is also the ink I add to make colored gloss coats out of the Dimensional Magic, Diamond Glaze and 3-D Crystal Lacquer, mentioned one page 11. For a wonderful watercolor look to your stamped image, you can paint the color directly onto a bold stamp and then stamp onto paper. This will give a very mottled, loose and painterly look to your image—more so than applying the brush markers directly to the stamp and then huffing on them. Depending on your stamp, it may be nice to add a loose pen-and-ink outline to the final, stamped image.

Permanent ink

Permanent ink is for nonporous surfaces. Stamp pads are available for this type of ink. The inkpads for the permanent ink get rock hard when dry, so rather than worry about that, use a piece of felt and a plastic plate to make a disposable pad for the project, then toss it out when you're finished. If you have to quit what you are working on for some reason, say to sleep, you can store the inkpad in a sealed plastic bag for a day or two.

Pigment inks

In addition to re-inking your pads, they are great for applying ink to glass for monoprinting and for sponging directly on your paper or clay project. Remember: These inks will not dry on gloss-coated paper without embossing. They will not even dry on matte paper if applied too thickly.

EMBOSSING POWDERS

PICTURED ARE A FEW DIFFERENT COL-ORS OF EMBOSSING POWDERS. THERE ARE CLEAR POWDERS, METALLIC POW-DERS, COLORED CONFETTI POWDERS AND GLITTER POWDERS, JUST TO LIST A FEW. I USE ALL POWDERS INTERCHANGEABLY, MIXING MY OWN CONCOCTIONS AS NEEDED. DON'T BE AFRAID TO MIX YOUR CUSTOM COLORS AS WELL. YOU DON'T EVEN NEED TO BUY SPECIAL LITTLE JARS FOR YOUR MIXES. A SMALL PLASTIC BAG WILL DO JUST FINE FOR STORAGE.

Embossing powders are applied to your decorative surface in many ways. You can shake them onto images stamped in pigment inks; or into pigment ink applied directly to the paper; or onto strips of double-stick tape. In other words, you want a tacky surface onto which the powder can stick until heated. The powder can be heated in a little broiler or toaster oven with the card face up or with a hair dryer and a lot of time. Even an iron turned upside down with the paper laid on it will work, which is what we did in the old days. But a heat gun is the fastest, most effective way to melt embossing powder, and it's well worth the investment.

➥

THIS *little papier-maché box was collaged with torn papers. The thin chipboard star was collaged, then triple embossed with Ultra Thick Embossing Enamel. Tiny beads from JudiKins were sprinkled into the warm powder and a wire wrap was added after the powder had cooled down.*

COLOR APPLICATION

Kid's paintbrush *

For stippling color from a dye inkpad onto paper, I use a large kid's paintbrush made by Crayola. It is a nice, soft, dense brush that is rounded, slightly feathered and well suited for stippling. Use one brush for each color of inkpad so you don't contaminate all your pads and brushes.

Dye brush markers *

Dye brush markers come in all shapes and sizes. I like these Impress markers from Tsukineko because they come in many colors and have a brush marker on one end and a bullet tip on the other. These are used to color directly onto the rubber before stamping or to color directly onto your project.

Markers *

A variety of markers for slick surfaces will serve you well for coloring metal, plastic and other nonporous (slick) surfaces.

Gel pens *

The metallic and opaque gel pens are great for coloring projects and adding detail work to stippled images.

Beads *

Tiny beads found in most stamp stores make a pretty and decorative addition to many projects.

Colored pencils *

Of course, you will want to have a variety of colored pencils on hand.

Metallic markers *

The last items are actually my favorite metallic markers. They are ultrametallic and work well on paper, clay or slick surfaces such as metal and plastic. Distributed by Krylon, these pens can be found in most stamp stores, fabric stores or hardware stores.

Acrylic paint cleanup

Wash acrylic paint off your stamps with soap and water using a soft toothbrush. A helpful hint about dried acrylic paint: Soak brushes or stamps for a few minutes (rubber part only—try not to soak the wood part of a stamp—ever!) in alcohol, and the paint will peel right off.

GLUES *and* ADHESIVES

THIS IS CERTAINLY NOT A COMPLETE LIST OF ADHESIVES, BUT THESE ARE THE PRODUCTS THAT WORK BEST FOR ME. NO SINGLE ADHESIVE IS GOOD FOR ALL THINGS, SO YOU'LL NEED TO EXPERIMENT. TRY THEM AND SEE WHAT WORKS FOR YOU.

YOU SHOULD KNOW WHETHER OR NOT PRODUCTS ARE PERMANENT FOR THE SOLE PURPOSE OF ADDING VALUE TO YOUR WORK. IF YOU ARE MAKING A QUICK GREETING CARD YOU DON'T NEED TO BE AS CONCERNED ABOUT PERMANENCE AS YOU WOULD BE WHEN YOU'RE SELLING A PIECE OF ART. A BUYER ALWAYS HAS THE RIGHT TO EXPECT PURCHASED ART TO LAST FOR MANY YEARS.

For speedy projects ✳

For quick assembly, I use double-stick Scotch tape, Wonder Tape or Miracle Tape—the last two tapes are found in most stamp stores. All of these tapes have good adhesion, but keep in mind that Scotch tape dries out over time and cannot be considered permanent. Also, Scotch tape will melt when heat is applied; the other two will not, so they may do double duty for embossing straight edges. Another product that I use when speed is required is the Super 77 spray adhesive from 3M. The adhesion is good for most papers, although it can be tricky to reposition, so only use this when you are sure of your placement.

Spray mount and rubber cement (not pictured) are both considered nonpermanent since they dry out over long periods of time. They may also lose their grip more rapidly on items stored in a hot area such as an attic or garage.

Rubber cement ✳

Many people don't know that rubber cement can be used as a temporary bond: If you coat one side of your work, let dry and stick it down, it will be temporary like a Post-it Note. If you want a permanent bond, you must coat both pieces to be bonded, let dry and then stick them together. It is also important that you brush it on both pieces in the same direction so you don't get a lot of little air pockets when you join the two together.

Glue ✳

YES! Glue is an excellent adhesive for both paper and charms in various materials. It can be considered a permanent adhesive even though it is water-soluble after it's dry. It dries clear, but on most dark papers it will dry shiny, so you should dab away any excess glue with a wet wipe. It usually will come up with water even after it's dry. It is relatively thick because the moisture content is low to keep paper from curling. If it's absolutely necessary to add water, only add a tiny bit.

For both rubber cement and YES! glue, use a piece of chipboard or plastic to spread it over large areas such as book covers. It will go a lot faster than using a paintbrush.

Perfect Paper Adhesive ✳

This is a favorite product of mine and is considered permanent. I use this product almost exclusively for decoupage. You'll probably need to water it down just a little to avoid a milky appearance when you decoupage over clear acrylic or glass such as jewelry boxes or plates. Use a paintbrush to apply it to the front and back of the piece to be glued, and smooth it down with the brush or with your hands. The moisture content is high and the

glue quickly absorbs into just about any paper, making it extremely malleable. This is a fantastic feature for decoupaging beads, plastic dolls heads and other three-dimensional items. It also sticks to all of the surfaces that I've tried, which is a definite plus. Also, it isn't sticky to the touch, which means you don't end up with all kinds of papers stuck to your hands if you work the way I do.

Glue stick *

Glue sticks are portable and easy to use in classes because they are less messy than, say, an open tub of YES! glue. Of all the glue sticks that I've tried, UHU is my favorite, but any of them will work just fine. The secret to making glue sticks work is to get an even coating and put enough on. Usually people put too little glue on the paper.

Gel super glue *

Quick Grab and any of the gel super glues work well to glue shrink plastic to other plastic, wood or metal.

Zap-A-Gap *

Zap-A-Gap (not pictured) is my favorite product for use with polymer clays and other plastics. The cyanoacrylates in both the glue and the clay will meld together, making a very strong joint.

Fray Check *

Fray Check stops the ends of ribbons and fabric from fraying. I also put a dab over knots to make sure they do not come untied. This product is available in most fabric stores.

Aleene's "Tacky" Glue *

Aleene's "Tacky" Glue works great for Victorian collage or assemblage or for when you need a glue that dries quickly. It dries flexible, so it is great for attaching brass charms and other slick-surfaced items to your art. The flexibility will allow the metals, in particular, to contract and expand without the items popping off. It's also considered permanent.

Glue application *

Have you ever noticed that the edges of your cardstock don't bond as well as the center? Most people apply glue, especially glue sticks, from the center out. Instead, apply the glue from the edges inward. Be sure to get a smooth, even, complete coverage with the glue. As you work toward the center, the edges have more time to become tacky. Just before joining the two pieces, give a quick retouch around the edges and your cardstock will stay down just fine. Another reason for a weak glue bond is that if you leave blank spots where there should be glue, those spots will help pull the bond apart as your project dries and contracts. Be sure to apply a good, smooth, even coat of glue, and then use the heat of your hands to help set the glued piece before moving on to the next step.

↑ HERE's *a book covered with a piece of mono-printed paper that has also been stamped and embossed with stamps from DeNami, Clearsnap and JudiKins. The center embellishment is a piece of paper coated with various colors of embossing powders and surrounded with a ring of "Tacky" Glue and copper embossing powder. The interior heart is made with shelf liner and embossing powder, with added beads. The metal leaf is from an old necklace.*

hint

Tacky glue I like to use Aleene's "Tacky" Glue when I'm gluing anything to foamcore. It grabs quickly and makes a great bond.

decorative surface embellishments

*1. **Color blocks** This was decorated by placing the Mini Vivid dye ink pads directly onto white cardstock and pressing lightly to get a rectangular impression of the ink in varying colors. Images in contrasting colors were randomly stamped over the color blocks. Stamped and embossed images, such as stars, would add even more texture and interest to the final paper. (Stamps are from eraser carvings by author.) *2. **Metallic pens** This was made by stamping alternating blocks of black and scarlet Vivid dye ink and completed by loosely drawing with Krylon metallic gilding pens. (Stamps are from eraser carvings by author.) *3. **Random pattern** Here I simply stamped coordinating images in different colors all over the paper. I did this quickly without masking. Overlapping the images adds interest. Use a stipple brush and Vivid stamp pads to randomly color the background for a soft airbrushed look. Colored pencils may be used to add color and detail. I added a little glitz with purple and gold spray webbing and, while the webbing was still wet, pressed gold and silver foil (found in stamp stores) onto the paper. (Stamps are from Acey-Deucy, DeNami and PSX.)

*4. **Paste paper** Make a very textural and interesting paper by mixing water into pre-mixed wallpaper paste (found in most hardware stores) and then adding acrylic paint. The mixture should be the consistency of very heavy cream. Use a sponge brush to apply the paste to dry paper. Use combs and stamps to lift off the paste for designs. Think about sponging on various colors at one time and then combing in your design. (Stamps are from Judikins.)

*5. **Paste Paper type 2** This was made by squirting metallic acrylic paint directly onto gloss coated cardstock and

Sample 3:
The addition of stamping and
embossing over the entire design

Sample 2:
Water, pens and spray webbing
with foil application

quickly smoothing with a sponge brush for an allover coating. Then the designs were combed in. If the paint is drying too fast to finish the designs, add an acrylic retarder to the paint. This product is found right next to the acrylic paints in most art stores. (No stamps, just combs were used.)

*6. **Marvey metallic markers** For the basic design, water was spritzed onto glossy cardstock. Then Marvey metallic markers were brushed over the wet paper, more water was spritzed, and so on until layers of color were built up. The more ink, the better the results, so don't be shy. Use a heat gun to move the ink around and to dry the paper. *7. **Art board collage** First seal the artboard (I use chipboard for artboard) with a coat of white gesso. This will prevent discoloration and yellowing of your art by preventing the binders in the board from leaching up into the paint and papers. The gesso will also keep your paint colors truer than if you start with a tan-colored chipboard or a colored mat board. When the gesso is dry, brush on random coats of acrylic paint. When the paint is dry, glue on strips of torn tissue and decorative papers. You may want to brush more paint over the glued papers. To build up the layered effect, stamp and emboss different images in different colors of ink and embossing powders. Think about adding a final layer of raised fabric paint in random patterns. Seal your work with a coat of Krylon Crystal Clear spray or your favorite sealant. (Stamps are from Acey-Deucy, embossed images were drawn freehand with embossing pen.)

monoprinting *with* PIGMENT INKS

MONOPRINTING IS AN OLD ARTFORM USED HERE WITH A NEW TWIST. ALL YOUR FRIENDS WILL ASK, "HOW DID YOU DO THAT?" IN TRADITIONAL MONO-PRINTING YOU USE PRINTER'S INKS. AS A RABID STAMPER, I LIKE TO SUBSTITUTE PIGMENT INKS. THE RESULTING IMAGERY IS INCREDIBLY INTERESTING AND GOES A LONG WAY TOWARD ENHANCING STAMP-ING PROJECTS. I USE MY DECORATED PA-PERS AS CARDS, ENVELOPES, WRAPPING PAPER, COLLAGE PIECES, AND BOOK COV-ERS—AND THAT'S JUST THE BEGINNING. MONOPRINTING IS SO CALLED BECAUSE IT IS A SIMPLE PRINTING METHOD THAT YIELDS ONE PRINT FOR EACH INKING OF THE GLASS. EACH PRINT WILL BE UNIQUE. AS YOU PROGRESS, YOU WILL THINK OF MANY USES FOR THESE DECO-RATED PAPERS.

Set aside a block of time, about three or four hours, to make as many decorated papers as you can without worrying about how you will use them. When you need a quick card or a wonderfully decorated envelope, go through your papers and "Voila!" Something cool will always be on hand.

So roll up your sleeves and get ready for some experimenting. Be bold and try every-thing. If at first you don't love something, keep it anyway. You may find a use for it to-morrow or next week.

WHAT YOU'LL NEED

* a piece of glass or Plexiglas at least 1" (2.5cm) larger on all sides than the piece of paper.

* several different colors of paper with a smooth surface both in text weight and cover stock — Chromecoat will not work, because the pigment ink will not dry on it. Linens and felts do not work well for me because the ink stays on top of the textured paper, which is not the look that I go for. Try it to see what I mean. It could very well create a subtle texture that you'll want to use. Start with lighter colors. The color of the paper will show through the print, so choose coordinating inks and papers.

* several colors of the pigment ink refill bottles — The colors print a little more mellow than they look, so experiment with different ones to find your personal preference.

* several stamps — The solid or heavier line stamps work best for me.

* brayer — I use a 4" (10cm) brayer.

* cosmetic sponges

* combs, cotton swabs, trowels and other objects for making decorative marks in the ink

Make a monoprint *

Start by slipping a piece of paper under your glass so you know how large to make the inked area. I generally use a 8½" x 11" sheet of paper so my inked area will be about 9"x12". You want it to completely cover the paper from edge to edge in order to get the best use out of the one print.

Using cosmetic sponges, ink the glass, starting with a few dots of pigment inks squeezed out all over the glass. Apply small dots at first until you find the correct amount for complete, light coverage. Change the sponges as you change ink colors. I use two or three colors on each plate. For instance, if I want a fall theme with turning leaves, I will use chianti, amber and maybe a hunter green. Blend the edges of the color patches, but do not overwork it so that it becomes muddy and loses the color separation. The colors will become slightly muted, which is what you want.

You need to achieve a nice, smooth coating of ink that is not too heavy or too light. If there is not enough ink on the plate, the print will be very pale. If there is too much, the print will be wet and gloppy and will not dry. Also, if there is too much ink, the design that you worked so hard to achieve will fuse together and be obliterated.

When you have a good, smooth inking you can make your design in several different ways. You can use combs to make spirals and lines, either wavy or straight, broken or meandering. You can also use cotton swabs or your fingers to draw in designs. Stamps can be used very effectively by stamping onto the glass and then stamping onto a blank sheet of text-weight paper to make a nice coordinating envelope paper for your card. While you are making your beautiful rainbow images on the envelope sheet, don't lose sight of the fact that your primary design is on the glass. When you are pretty sure that you have what you want (and believe me, you can never be completely positive), lay your paper firmly on the glass, making sure that it doesn't slide and smear. Roll the brayer over the back of the paper with a firm pressure. Be sure to cover every square inch three or four times at least. You want the design to transfer to the paper. Carefully lift off your paper and see what you have. Set it aside to dry a little and begin work on the next sheet.

Leave the ink residue on the plate, add a few more dots and re-ink as before. To be more economical, I gradually change colors so I don't have to wash any more ink than I have to down the drain. When you are done, just place the glass in the sink and run warm water over it or use a baby wipe to wipe it off. The sponges can be rinsed out, left to dry and reused, or they can be put in a small plastic bag, sealed and used later. The ink won't dry out on the sponges, and I don't like to waste it by rinsing unless the colors become too muddy.

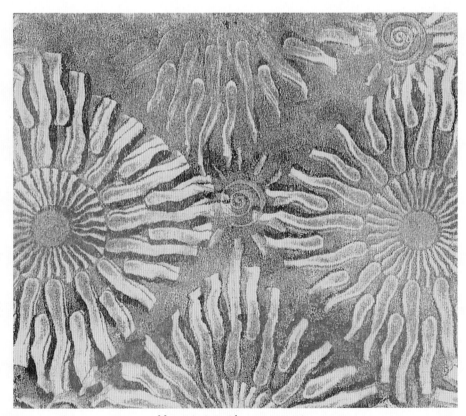

Monoprinting with no overstamping
(STAMPS: JUDIKINS)

monoprinting with pigment inks
|continued|

If at first you say, "Yuck! This isn't what I wanted," think again. You can now stamp and emboss more images on top to further embellish your paper. You can use different embossing powders to give it sparkle. You can use the next inking as a rainbow pad to stamp more images on top and leave them unembossed. You will probably cut up the sheet of paper to make several cards, so just a portion is actually used from each project. Remember, too, that little pieces work beautifully in collages. The final project will bear little resemblance to the raw sheet of monoprint, so chin up and keep plugging away. You'll be happy that you did when your friends, penpals and everyone else says, "Wow! How did you do that?"

Stamping and embossing added to the monoprint (STAMPS: DENAMI, STAMP FRANCISCO, AMERICAN ART STAMP)

Cutting paper

If you are cutting paper to be the text block for a book, you will probably–depending on the format of the book–want the text block to have very straight, very even edges. The best way to ensure this is to take a ream of paper to your nearest print shop and they will usually cut it for you in whatever measurement you like. They all have nominal charges per cut so ask what their rates are BEFORE they cut the paper.

The place that you buy your chipboard will also cut it for you, but chances are your chipboard will not have to be cut perfectly. Chances are you will do a fine job with a straight ede and a utility knife.

To get a nice, straight edge on your chipboard or paper, the first and most important rule is to stand up. It doesn't matter if you are using a rotary cutter or a knife, you'll get far better results if you just stand up. Be sure that the blade in your knife is sharp. Lay your straight edge next to the cut line and hold it firmly in place with your non-cutting hand. Be sure to keep your fingers and knuckles out of the path of the blade! Draw the blade toward you being sure to keep it upright. If you don't stand up to cut, it will be too easy to get a messy, beveled edge in your project. With thicker chipboard, you will want to make a shallow cut and then make another and another until you are through the board. If you try to cut through the thick board all in one motion, it can cause you to slip out of line or get a beveled edge because you are pressing too hard with the knife. Do not cut chipboard with your rotary or guillotine cutter. The resin binding agent will dull your blade way too fast when you consider how much you paid for your paper cutter blades.

making an envelope
without a template

ALTHOUGH YOU CAN CERTAINLY BUY TEMPLATES FOR A WIDE VARIETY OF ENVELOPE STYLES AND SIZES, IT IS USEFUL TO KNOW HOW TO MAKE AN ENVELOPE THAT WILL FIT ANY SIZE OR SHAPE CARD THAT YOU MAY MAKE. AN ENVELOPE CAN BE MADE OF ANY PAPER, OF COURSE, BUT IT'S MOST SATISFYING TO MAKE ENVELOPES OUT OF PAPERS THAT YOU DECORATE YOURSELF.

WHAT YOU'LL NEED

* *paper — I usually use 8½" x 11" since it is an easy size to work with and it fits most of my cards*
* *double-stick tape or glue*
* *scissors*
* *finished card to measure for sizing the envelope*

1] Lay your card on the paper so that you can fold up from the bottom and still have an ample flap for the closure. Crease the paper well.

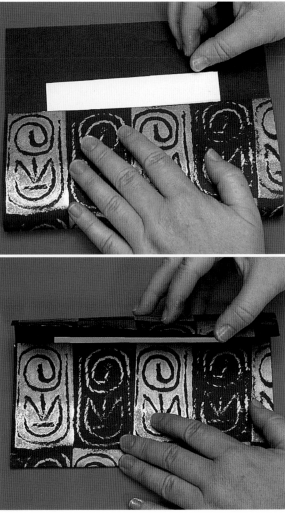

2] Fold the top flap down and crease well.

making an envelope without a template
| continued |

3] Open the paper out and fold the sides in, still following the card configuration and crease well.

4] Now open the paper out flat so that you can see all the crease lines.

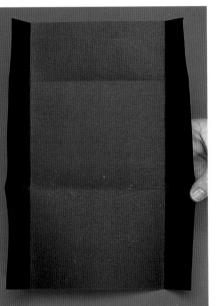

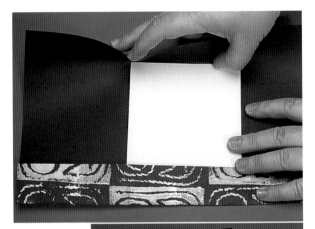

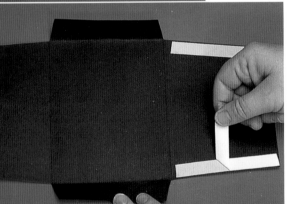

5] Snip the corners out of the paper at a slight angle.

6] Seal the side edges with double stick tape or glue.

making a custom stamp

PENSCORE, A PRODUCT SOLD BY CLEARSNAP, IS FOUND AT MOST STAMP STORES. THIS FOAM-LIKE MATERIAL, WHEN HEATED, HOLDS A VERY DE-TAILED IMPRESSION OF AN ITEM THAT HAS BEEN PRESSED INTO IT. AFTER THE PENSCORE COOLS FOR A FEW SECONDS, THE ITEM IS RE-MOVED, CREATING A GREAT CUSTOM STAMP.

WHEN CREATING PAPER DESIGNS, IT'S USEFUL TO HAVE A REVERSE IMAGE OF AN EXISTING STAMP. JUST PRESS THE RUBBER STAMP ONTO THE HEATED PENSCORE, AND IT WILL MAKE A REVERSE-IMAGE STAMP TO USE IN YOUR DESIGNS.

WHAT YOU'LL NEED
* piece of twine
* block of wood or acrylic
* piece of Penscore cut to the same size as the wood or acrylic block
* piece of chipboard cut to the same size as the wood block
* tacky glue and white glue
* heat gun
* piece of felt
* plastic plate
* ink for stamping — here I'm using metallic ink from Zim so the design will show up well on my black paper

1] Use the white glue to draw a design on the chipboard. Work freehand, or draw a design and trace it with the glue.

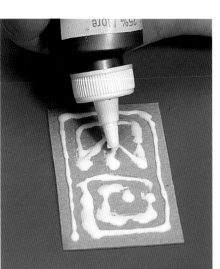

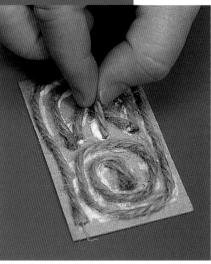

2] Cut pieces of twine and lay them onto the glue as shown.

MAKING A CUSTOM STAMP
| continued |

3] After the glue dries, use double-stick tape to attach the chipboard with the design on it to the block. Now you have a positive stamp.

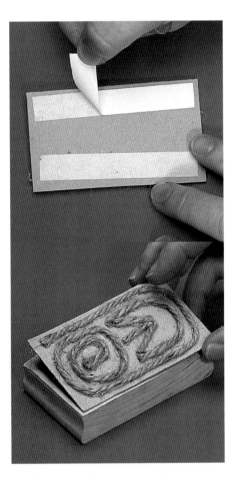

4] Heat the Penscore with the heat gun for a minute, then impress your positive image onto it.

5] Attach the Penscore to the back side of the block to make a negative stamp. You may want to use two pieces of wood to keep your hands cleaner while you stamp.

6] Make a disposable rainbow inkpad by applying different colors in a striped pattern. Here I've used copper, gold and silver ink. Ink the stamp.

7] Stamp in alternating blocks, leaving room for the image from the other side of your stamp.

8] Now ink the reverse stamp and fill in the gaps to create an attractive design on your paper.

fancy fan
book

This little book is a fun and fast project that is great for gift giving or selling at craft fairs. You can decorate the text block (the tags) with art or with writing, or you can give or sell this as a blank book. Your friends and customers will be thrilled with it either way. This book also looks great with metallic tape on the edges instead of the embossed tape.

MATERIALS

FAN

* eight shipping tags for the text block
* one piece of styrene or other plastic for the clear cover—I've used a piece that is 0.05" (1.3mm) thick
* one piece of colored cardstock for the collage backing
* one piece of chipboard for the back cover— again, I've used a 0.05" thickness
* one yard (one meter) each of four or five different fancy fibers
* two-holed plain button for the back
* one fancy button for the front
* doily
* metal transfer foil

OTHER ART SUPPLIES

* heart stamp and text stamp
* tapestry needle
* stipple brush
* colored pencils
* watercolors
* dye inkpads
* waterproof ink and a brush
* gold embossing powder
* Sailor Rolling Ball Glue Pen
* glue stick
* embossable double-stick tape (Wonder or Miracle Tape, not Scotch)
* Fray Check
* paper punch
* plastic-cutting knife
* drill with ¼" (6mm) bit

2] Cut one piece of cardstock and one piece of plastic exactly the same size as the chipboard back. I use styrene so that I can use a pair of old scissors to cut it. Metal shears also work great on styrene. Scissors may chip acrylic and Plexiglas, so you will need to use a plastic-cutting knife for them. You can use a paper punch to punch the holes out of the chipboard and the paper, but you'll have to use a drill to drill a hole into the plastic. I use a regular hand drill with a ¼" (6mm) drill bit.

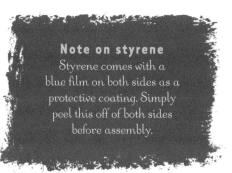

Note on styrene
Styrene comes with a blue film on both sides as a protective coating. Simply peel this off of both sides before assembly.

1] Use a utility knife and a straightedge to cut a piece of chipboard a little larger than the shipping tags. A ¼" (6mm) margin on three sides would be appropriate. Make the top edge flush with the tags.

3] To start this collage, color a doily with watercolor washes.

4] Stamp your images in waterproof ink and color them with watercolors and/or colored pencils. Don't be afraid to paint over the lines. It'll give a prettier look to your project. Use colored pencils to add detail if you wish.

5] Stipple straw-colored Vivid! dye ink to antique the torn-text stamping. I like to use the Crayola kid's paintbrushes for stippling. They are readily available and inexpensive. Use a different brush for each color family to avoid contaminating your dye stamp pads.

6] To assemble your collage, use a glue stick and start applying the layers to the background cardstock.

7] Add the doily and the stamped, colored cutouts to your collage.

8] Use the Sailor Rolling Ball Glue Pen to apply small dots of glue to the places where you want to apply the foil. This glue comes out of the tube blue and dries completely clear. This is a two-way glue so that when the coat is dry it will still be tacky, like a Post-it Note.

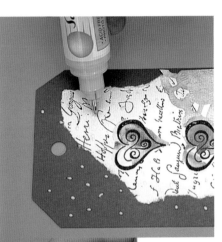

9] Place the foil, dull side down, onto the completely dry dots of glue. Rub the foil to make good contact with the glue and peel up the foil paper.

10] Run a fine line of glue stick onto the edges of your collage and place the clear plastic on top.

11] Run a length of double-stick tape around the edges of the sandwiched front cover.

12] Snip the corner edges of the tape on the front and the back of the cover.

13] Fold one edge of the tape over the cover and press down well. (If you don't press the edges down very well, embossing powder may get under them and prevent the tape from sticking to the cover.) Peel off the paper backing one edge at a time so that you don't trap your paper under the previous edge's tape. You can miter the corners if you wish.

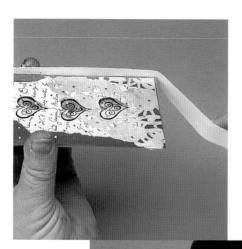

14] Pour the embossing powder onto a sheet of scratch paper and lay the taped edges over it to pick up the powder. Press well to get the powder to stick all over the tape. Use a soft paintbrush to brush off the excess powder. Heat each edge and then wave the piece around a little to cool it off. Continuous heat may cause the plastic to warp. Remember not to aim the gun at your fingers. If the plastic gets too hot for you to handle, hold it with a pair of pliers during embossing.

15] To assemble the book, thread a needle with a length of matching fiber and run it through one side of the back button, up through the chipboard, the tags, the cover, and the fancy button; then back down through the stack.

16] Tie off the back thread with a square knot.

17] Use Fray Check to secure the knot firmly and trim the ends off to about ¹⁄₂" (12mm).

18] Slip the braided hang tassel (instructions on opposite page) under the fancy button on the front cover. The pressure of the tied button will hold the tassel in place just fine.

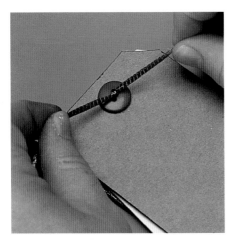

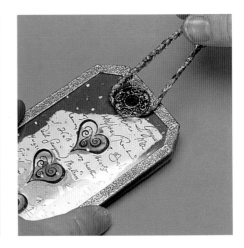

Tassel assembly

My drawing shows the tie of the cord at the top of the tassel. For this fan book, position the knot so that it will be buried in the bulb of the tassel above the wrapped neck.

add the tassel

1] Wrap fibers around a piece of chip-board. I wrapped five strands around the board eight times. Wrap as many times as you like, which will determine how full your tassel will be.

2] Tie a cord around and under the tassel.

3] Slip the fibers off the chipboard and cut them at the ends.

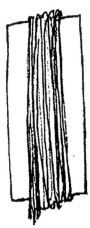

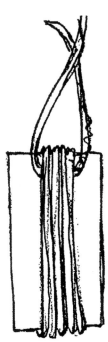

4] Hold a length of fiber next to the tassel as shown, making a loop at the top and leaving a little tail. Note the color of the tail. You will have to find it again in a minute.

5] Wrap the fiber around the loop, catching it securely, and continue to wrap up toward the loop.

6] Slip the tail of the wrapped cord into the loop, find the original tail and give a little tug downward. You want to pull the original loop and the final tail into the wrapped neck of the tassel to hide the ends.

a SIMPLE
album

This little album is probably the easiest book that I know how to make. This project is excellent for the times when you need a fast gift that can be for anyone, young or old, male or female. The chipboard can be covered with decorative paper or left natural as shown. The overall impact can easily be shifted with just a small change in the colors and materials used.

MATERIALS

ALBUM
* one piece of chipboard for the back, cut to the size you wish the final book to be (pictured book is 5¾ " x 7" [14.6cm x 17.8cm])
* one piece of chipboard cut to the size of the front spine (in this case, 1" x 5¾" [2.5cm x 14.6cm])
* one piece of rubber cut the same size as the back piece of chipboard (I buy the rubber from a hardware store)
* text-weight paper for pages
* two screw posts, ½" (12mm) in length or whatever height you like (you can get the screw posts at stationery stores or hardware stores)
* a medallion for the front cover (mine is made of polymer clay and stamped with an image from Clearsnap)

OTHER ART SUPPLIES
* Quick Grab glue
* two-hole paper punch

1] Use a regular two-hole paper punch to punch out the holes for the screw posts. Insert the posts facing up from the back cover.

2] Lay your punched stack of text-weight papers onto the posts.

3] Lay the punched rubber sheet on top of the text block.

4] Lay the spine piece on top of the rubber.

5] Place the screws into position and tighten them. A screwdriver or a penny may be of help in tightening the screws, but the screws should go into the posts with minimal effort. If they are hanging up, back them out and try again. You don't want to strip the threads by forcing them.

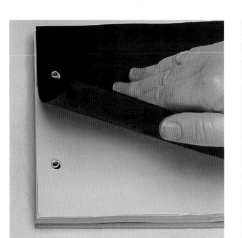

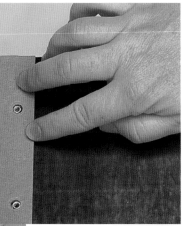

6] Use the Quick Grab glue to set the medallion in place. See page 91 for instructions for using polymer clay.

See page 91 for instructions for using polymer clay.

hint

This book is shown with a paperclay medallion layered over a piece of burned copper, then a piece of screen. **Quick Grab glue** is good for holding these different items together.

perfect PRESENTATION
display box

If you would like to make the most of an item, consider its presentation. This attractive box that folds shut to resemble a book turns a "very nice" creation into an "oh wow!" creation. It is easy to assemble and can be made as simple or as ornate as you like. With lots of room for stamp art in the process, this is a fun and easy little addition to just about anything you want to present or display. I use this form of presentation when I want to give added importance to trinkets, memorabilia and other small items. The box can be made to any size and, by adding layers of foamcore, to any display depth. For this project I have listed the dimensions in the supplies list, but do keep in mind that you will want to make your book the size required to house your treasures.

MATERIALS

DISPLAY BOX

* two equal size pieces of chipboard or mat board for the front and back cover (I used 0.100" [1.3cm] plain gray chipboard cut to 4" x 4" [10cm x 10cm])

* two pieces of ¼" (6mm) thick foamcore cut to the appropriate size, or

* one piece of ½" (12mm) thick foamcore (I used ¼" [6mm] foamcore cut to 3⅞" x 3⅞" [9.8cm x 9.8cm]. All you need to remember is that the foamcore should be ⅛" [3mm] smaller than the covers so nothing peeks out.)

* decorative paper for the covers, any kind

* one piece of black text-weight paper large enough to cover your foamcore frame

* two pieces of black paper for liner, each cut to about 3¾" x 3¾" (9.5cm x 9.5cm)

* black cloth tape, such as book tape or black gaffer's tape

* ⅝" (16mm) grosgrain ribbon for the book wrap (I used one piece cut to approximately 10" [25cm] and a little piece cut to 3" [7.6cm])

* ⅝" (16mm) D-ring

* one brass eyelet and a setting tool

* self-stick hook-and-loop tape

OTHER ART SUPPLIES

* tacky glue, glue stick and white glue

* Fray Check

* black felt-tip pen

2] This is a mock-up of me cutting out the frame, but I always use a straightedge to cut a straight line (oops!). With foamcore you need a very sharp blade to keep the foam from bunching up. Also, don't try to cut through the entire thickness in one swoop, especially if you're cutting the thicker foamcore. Expect to make a cut through the first half and then follow up with a second slice to break through the bottom sheet of paper.

3] If using ¼" (6mm) foamcore, use tacky glue to glue two pieces of foamcore together, making a frame that is ½" (12mm) deep. Be sure to smooth out those lumps of glue for a nice bond.

1] Cut a piece of foamcore to your specifications. Measure and mark the corners for a frame that is ½" (12mm) wide.

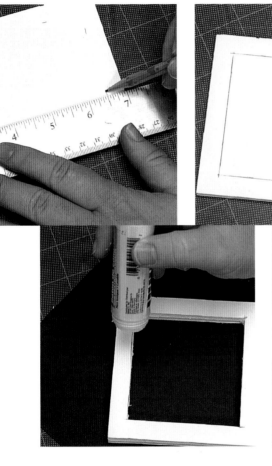

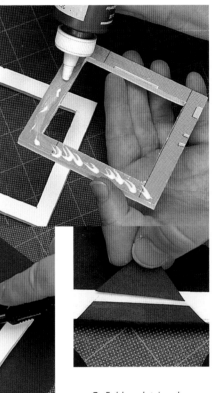

6] Fold each triangle-shaped paper upward and trim off the points so that the paper covers the back but doesn't peek out past the outside edge.

4] *Far left:* Use a glue stick to coat one side of the frame.

5] Place the frame in the center of the black text-weight paper, turn it over and smooth out any wrinkles. Remember to use the heat of your hands to help speed the drying time. Flip the assembly back over and cut an X on the black paper from corner to corner inside the frame.

hint

Gaffer's tape Gaffer's tape is found in photo or television studio supply houses. It is a coated fabric tape that has low tack, so when you lay it down lightly and it isn't positioned perfectly, you can peel it up easily without ripping your paper. After you press it down firmly, it stays in place. It is also nonreflective, which makes it perfect and pretty for this project.

7] Cut little corner covers from a piece of the same black paper, fold them and use white glue to glue them snugly into place.

8] Cut a little snip into the corner cover down to the frame corner. Use tacky glue to lay the corner pieces down on the back side of the frame.

9] Use tacky glue to glue the little triangles up into place.

10] Cut the ends of the frame cover, making tabs as shown.

11] Use tacky glue to secure the tabbed length of the frame cover, wrapping the tabs around the corners of the frame. Cut a little slit and glue the overlapping edges down into place.

12] Trim the finishing edges and glue into position.

⬆ THIS *is what the final frame looks like from the front.*

14] Place the cover in the center of your decorative paper and glue it down. Flip it over, smooth it and dry the glue stick with the heat of your hands. Along the edges of the cover, make a crease in the decorative paper between two fingers. This will make the edges of your book look extra sharp.

13] Coat the cover with glue stick. Make sure you get a nice, full coverage leaving no portion of the chipboard unglued.

15] Glue down the two opposite edges and use your fingernail or a bone folder to really smash down the ends that will be turned under.

16] For this lightweight paper, these pinched and folded corners will do fine. When you pinch the corners in, be sure to keep the edges of the paper a little off the edges of the cover as shown. If you pull the fold in too close, it will make a bulky corner. Remember that there are no right or wrong corner-folding methods, just good choices for the materials involved. You may want to use a different corner method if your cover material is too thick to make a relatively flat corner using this technique.

17] Cut a strip of tape a little longer than the board and lay it sticky side up. Place the covers about ⅞" (22mm) apart, putting an equal amount of tape on either side. Sometimes it's easier for my students to line up the tape and boards on a cutting mat with gridlines. To determine the width of the spine tape, you must consider the depth of your frame piece and add about ⅜" (10mm) to allow for the added thickness of your chipboard and tape.

18] Fold the excess tape edges down, making sure that you do not close up the spine width by taping straight across. You must ease the tape ends down into the valley and crease it to the inside of the cover board edge.

19] Cut a piece of tape just a little shorter than the covers and lay it down, starting on one side and creasing it in toward the cover edge as shown.

20] Continue laying the tape down into the valley, creasing as you go. Remember: A straight fold across will close up the spine width, and you don't want to do that.

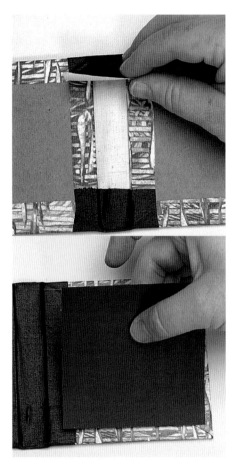

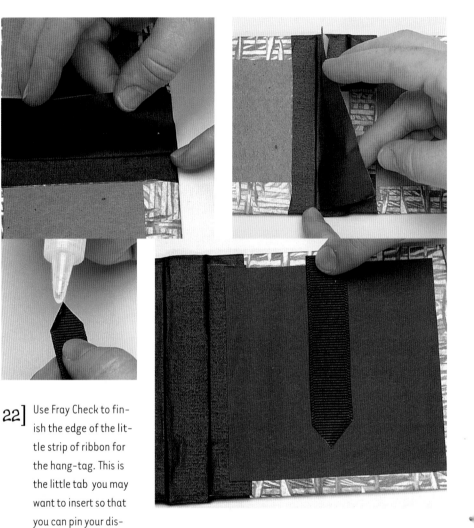

21] Glue the liner papers into place on the front and back covers.

22] Use Fray Check to finish the edge of the little strip of ribbon for the hang-tag. This is the little tab you may want to insert so that you can pin your display items onto it. This is, of course, optional.

23] Use white glue to place the tag into position.

24] Use a black felt-tip pen to hide any unsightly white edges that may show on your tape.

25] Use tacky glue for good adhesion of the frame to the back cover board.

26] Fold the wrapper (in this case, the longer ribbon) onto the D-ring and secure it with a dab of white glue. Cut a tiny slit and insert the eyelet. Remember not to go wild with the blade—the opening has to be small enough to hold the eyelet.

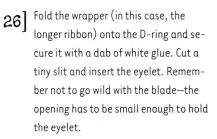

27] Set the eyelet with the setter. Finish the pointed edge of the ribbon with Fray Check.

28] Use the tacky glue to adhere the ribbon wrap to the back side of the book.

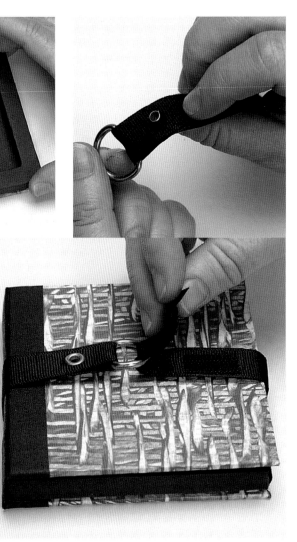

29] Bring the wrap around, thread it through the D-ring to get correct position and then adhere the self-stick pieces of hook-and-loop tape.

DOWEL-SPINED
book

This arty little book is simple enough for a

child to make, but sophisticated enough for

an adult to appreciate. The construction is a

little different because of the use of a simple

dowel for a spine. A little creative thinking

will yield lots of other objects that can be

used as a spine. Think about a small

wooden spoon for an original cookbook, a large nail for an industrial

look or twigs for an earthy look. The options are many, making this an exciting book with

lots of possibilities. The scratchboard adds a beautiful cover—sophisticated and simple to do.

MATERIALS

FOR BOOK
* two pieces of chipboard cut approximately
  5⅝" x 5¾" (14.3cm x 14.6cm)
* 20 sheets of text-weight paper cut to
  11" x 5½" (28cm x 14cm)
* ¼" (6mm) dowel cut to 5" (12cm) length
* two black sheets of cover stock cut to
  5½" x 5½" (14cm x 14cm) for liner
* two sheets of decorative papers for the front
  and back covers (I used a cream text-weight
  paper and an Acey Deucy text stamp)
* assorted fancy fibers

* two wooden beads with holes large enough to
  get the fibers through
* scratchboard for cover

OTHER ART SUPPLIES
* scratchboard tools
* embossing ink and powders
* awl
* tapestry needle
* brush markers
* Fray Check
* sandpaper

1] Cut a piece of scratchboard larger than your intended book cover. Stamp in a random pattern and emboss with different colors of embossing powder. Here I used a Moe Wubba heart stamp, a Hero Arts leaf stamp and a Gains & McCall dot stamp. I always make extra of the same pattern so I can use the leftover portion for cards, gift tags, pins and other pretties.

2] Use the scratch tools or a nail to scratch in little lines and hash marks around the stamped image.

3] Color the revealed white paper with brush markers.

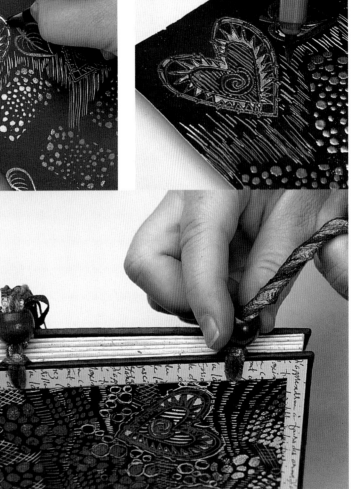

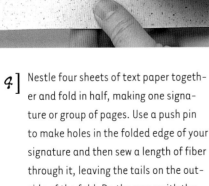

4] Nestle four sheets of text paper together and fold in half, making one signature or group of pages. Use a push pin to make holes in the folded edge of your signature and then sew a length of fiber through it, leaving the tails on the outside of the fold. Do the same with the rest of the paper so you have five signatures with fibers through them.

5] After you have covered and lined the front and back book covers use an awl to punch holes through them. Thread a few fibers through these holes with a slipknot. Place all five signatures between the book covers, gather all the fibers and twist them as shown. Feed the fibers into the bead by twisting the bead on in the same direction as the fibers are twisted.

6] After you've sanded the ends of the dowel smooth, you can color it with a marker or paint and let it dry.

7] Divide the fibers in half and place the dowel on top of them. Tie a square knot over the dowel at each end of the book.

Finishing touches
If your fibers are slippery, you may want to consider fixing the knots with Fray Check. The last step on this book was to thread assorted beads onto the ends of the hanging fibers.

⬆ **HERE** *is a collaged card made with an excess piece of the scratchboard and a piece of the stamped cover paper.*

• surprise
jewelry box

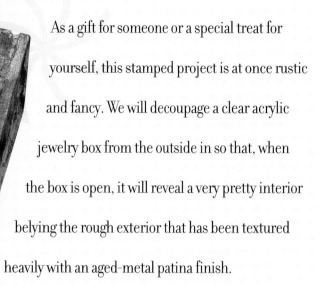

As a gift for someone or a special treat for

yourself, this stamped project is at once rustic

and fancy. We will decoupage a clear acrylic

jewelry box from the outside in so that, when

the box is open, it will reveal a very pretty interior

belying the rough exterior that has been textured

heavily with an aged-metal patina finish.

MATERIALS

JEWELRY BOX
* *inexpensive plastic box with lid*

OTHER ART SUPPLIES
* *metal patinas (I used Instant Iron with Instant Rust and Copper Topper with Patina Green from Modern Options)*

* *various stamps to make a page of stamped images in waterproof ink (all the images here are from Acey Deucy)*

* *stipple brush*

* *dye ink pads*

* *colored pencils*

* *black acrylic paint*

* *Perfect Paper Adhesive*

* *paintbrush for the glue*

* *wrapping paper to cut images from if desired*

1] Stamp several images in waterproof ink on white paper. Use a stipple brush, the dye ink pads and the pencils to add color to the images.

2] Cut out the images and lay them face up to apply the Perfect Paper Adhesive with a paintbrush. I usually thin the adhesive with water to a thick cream consistency.

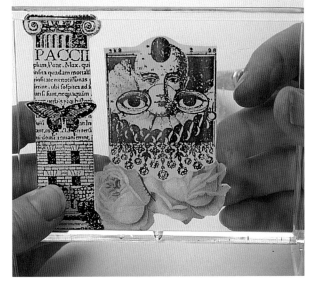

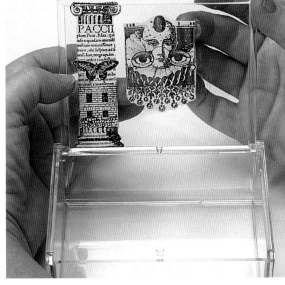

3] Apply the image onto the plastic, smoothing it out and drying it with your hands as you go. This is another place where I appreciate the nonstick feel of the Perfect Paper Adhesive to my hands. If it were any other decoupage medium, I would have all kinds of stuff stuck to me.

4] Continue applying images to the backs of the previously glued images. As you can see, we paste the focal-point images down first and then layer the others behind them for the background images. You're working backwards from what you would normally do on a collage. If you have trouble visualizing and working in this manner, cut a sheet of paper to size for each side of the box, glue your collage into place as you normally would, and then apply the entire collage to the plastic.

Final step

Coat the black acrylic paint with Copper Topper and let it dry. Brush on another coat, and while it's still tacky, add Patina Green. Let it dry to a pretty green and then randomly sponge on Instant Iron and then Instant Rust. Continue adding and alternating layers until you like it. You cannot hurry the drying time on the Patina Green with a heat gun: It will just stop the process and you will get very little green color. But you can hurry the rust process with the heat gun.

5] This is a view of the top portion of the lid. Paint the black acrylic paint all over your box and let it dry. Be sure to coat all the edges that will show when the box is closed. This top rim, for instance, should be painted, but the side edges that will go down into the closed box should not. Don't put acrylic paint on any surface that might touch and stick to another.

➡➤ THIS *box was the result of one of those happy accidents. I had glued everything down and then decided that there was just something that I was not thrilled with. I thought that if I soaked the box in warm water, I could remove the images from it. I started peeling off the layers of paper and discovered that Perfect Paper Adhesive was an excellent transfer agent, since I could not peel the remaining images off the plastic. I worked for a while, scratching a little off here and there with a scouring brush, and then decided that all this scratching wasn't going to make a nice, shiny surface on which to work a new design. It was at that point that I wondered what the image would look like if I coated the box with yellow, cream and black acrylic paints. I loved it! With its abstract look, it's now one of my favorite boxes.*

small stationery folio

Often you will want to give or sell a set of stationery cards, and what better way to present them than in a lovely and practical little stationery folio? These folios work great to house many other gifts as well. Do you need to give a set of photos, a CD, or maybe a gift of gloves and a scarf? As with all the projects in this book, this pattern is easy to tailor to the size of your particular contents and you can make it as simple or as embellished as you wish.

MATERIALS

FOLIO
* thin piece of chipboard or posterboard cut to the pattern provided on page 51
* sheet of decorative paper large enough to cover the chipboard or posterboard
* smaller decorative papers for the card and front decorations
* stationery cards and envelopes
* paper for liner

OTHER ART SUPPLIES
* 3M Super 77 spray adhesive
* clear nail polish (optional for the paper medallion on the front of your folio, should you use one)
* double-stick tape
* self-stick hook-and-loop tape or magnetic tape for the closure

1] Cut out and score the body of the folio on both sides. Remember that to make nice edges on the folds in chipboard, you must score with a knife on the outside and score with a stylus on the inside of the fold. Then, if you've scored deeply enough with the knife, it should be easy to make a clean fold. Cover the board evenly and entirely with permanent spray adhesive

2] Place the glued board onto the back side of the decorative paper cover and smooth it out. Use your knife to cut right up to the edges for a quick project.

Using the pattern
Note that when you cut out the decorative paper, you must refer to the pattern in the book to be sure to cut out an edge on each side of the paper. This is not really shown in the photographs, so don't forget. These side paper tabs will be folded over and glued to the chipboard side tabs.

3] Here the folio has been folded all the way up, with the side tabs tucked in. The side paper tabs are being glued to the chipboard tabs. I usually use a strip of double-stick tape for this part, but glue would work fine as well.

4] Use spray mount or glue to glue the liner into place.

Paste paper recipe
I use Methocel (methyl cellulose) to make paste paper. Mix one tablespoon of Methocel in two cups of hot water and stir well. Add one teaspoon of ammonia and stir again. The mix will thicken as soon as you add the ammonia. Let it set until the liquid turns clear. Add acrylic paints to color the Methocel, paint it onto smooth paper with a foam brush and use combs to comb the designs into the wet Methocel mix. See the resource section for more info on Methocel.

5] After the liner is positioned, carefully bend the front flap down, molding the liner into the crease.

6] Use a stylus to further define the crease.

7] Stick one side of the magnet (or hook-and-loop tape) in place on the flap and lay the second side in place, bringing the self-stick magnet down to its corresponding position on the front of the folio.

⬆ **decorate** *the front of the folio and the note cards as you like. I used a paperclay medallion on this one (see page 92 for paperclay instructions). The cards on the other version were made with strips and squares of decorative papers glued to cream cardstock.*

➤→

COPY this pattern onto heavy-weight cardstock or construction paper. The paper that I used is the packing from X-ray material. Posterboard would be a good alternative for this project.

Cut the box out on the solid lines. Glue the paste paper down to the board and smooth it really well. Trim the paper right up to the edges of the board. Use stamps to decorate the inside of the box.

Score with a stylus on the inside and fold the box on the dotted lines. Use tacky glue to glue the tabs together. Use self-stick magnets for the closure if you like.

Decorate the flap of the box as well as the stationery cards with pieces of chipboard, Dimensional Magic and paste paper scraps.

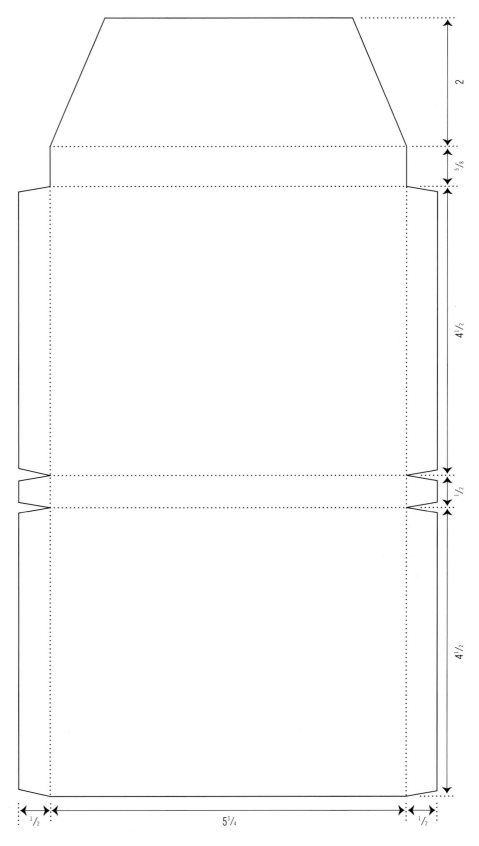

2

5/8

4 1/2

1/2

4 1/2

1/2   5 3/4   1/2

large
portfolio

This portfolio is the easiest to make and the most practical ever, which is exactly why it has become such a classic. Designed to house flat papers of assorted sizes, this portfolio is great for both storage and transportation. The covers on this particular project are shown stamped brightly on one version, but the step-by-step project is in black and white alone. We're making a slightly more complicated portfolio by adding a front flap for closure, but certainly, omitting the flap and ribbon tie leaves it every bit as useful and just as attractive. You know those really large sheets of paper that you buy, such as watercolor papers and marbled papers? Well, if you take two large sheets of heavy chipboard and tape them together at the side, insert your papers and wrap them securely with a common string tie, you can store your papers upright and tucked behind an armoire with no buckling problems. So you see, even the most pared down, meager portfolio of this type is able to pull its weight in usefulness.

MATERIALS

FOLIO
* two pieces of art board or chip-board covered in white paper and cut to equal sizes
* piece of chipboard for the front flap (optional) and self-stick magnetic tape for a closure
* black paper to line front flap
* two large sheets of paper for the inside pockets
* black 2" (5cm) wide gaffer's tape or book tape
* 1" (2.5cm) wide black tape for the trim (optional)

OTHER ART SUPPLIES
* YES! glue

1] Cut a length of the 2" (5cm) wide tape a little longer than the length of your covers. Lay it sticky side up and position the front and back covers on the tape, trying to get the front and back seams even. I usually make a spine of about ³/₄" to 1" (19mm to 25mm) but you can make the spine as wide or narrow as you like. If you need to store more papers, a wider spine is in order. My students often find it helpful to do this positioning on a cutting mat with a grid so that they can line up the edges of the covers. If you need to do this, but don't have a cutting mat large enough, line up the bottom edges of the covers along the table's edge to get them straight.

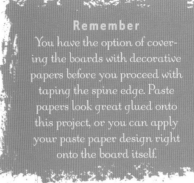

Remember
You have the option of covering the boards with decorative papers before you proceed with taping the spine edge. Paste papers look great glued onto this project, or you can apply your paste paper design right onto the board itself.

2] Fold the ends of the tape up and in.

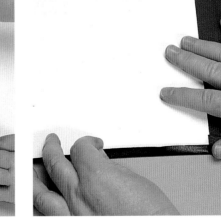

3] Cut a length of tape a little shorter than the portfolio and use it to cover the exposed tape.

4] This step shows the optional trim treatment with the narrower black tape.

5] Cover the front flap with black paper on both sides and attach it to the front cover with the black tape as shown.

6] Snip the tape and fold the edges in.

7] Cover the exposed tape with another piece of tape.

8] Use a piece of chipboard to spread YES! glue all across the front cover. The chipboard facilitates complete, fast coverage of the glue.

9] Cut the large black sheets of paper into liners that are, basically, a rectangle with four flaps to fold in, one on each side. Picture yourself cutting an envelope that will be glued to the board on the back side with the flaps left unglued, but tucked in. Position the liner onto the glued board and smooth it down. Remember to go over it well with your hands to smooth and dry the glue before going on to the next step.

10] Fold the edges of the liner up and into place. The liner flaps stay free for expansion to accept many papers easily. They are not glued down at all.

11] The final step is attaching the self-stick magnet to the front flap and front cover.

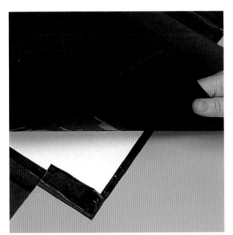

⬆ THE *finished portfolio without cover decoration.*

POCKET
portfolio

Here is another type of portfolio that is pretty and practical. You'll want to make this in several different sizes to house everything from cards to larger paper products. Try covering it with fabric—it'll look great! You can use YES! glue for fabric adhesion as well. The dimensions given on this project will allow the folio to contain 8½" x 11" papers nicely.

MATERIALS

PORTFOLIO

* piece of chipboard cut to 12" x 26" (30.5cm x 66cm) (I used the thinner chipboard for this project, but you can use any thickness that you have on hand)

* pattern provided on pages 60–61

* sheet of 8½" x 11" black text-weight paper

* decorative paper to cover the chipboard

* magnetic strips for the front closure

* a sheet of black 8½" x 11" cardstock

* black book tape or photographic blackout tape (optional trim)

OTHER ART SUPPLIES

* clips

* YES! glue

* something to decorate the front flap (optional—I'm using a paperclay medallion stamped with a sun for this project)

1] Transfer the pattern to the long piece of chipboard. Score one side of the board with a knife, the other side with a stylus. Fold the board in toward the stylus score. Cut off the flap portion and use paper tape to tape it back on, leaving a gap of about $\frac{1}{8}$" (3mm). You only need to tape one side. I decorated with a stamp from Stampers Anonymous and a little flower stamp from Hero Arts on yellow ochre wrapping paper.

2] Use a chipboard scrap to spread the YES! glue onto one section of the folio at a time.

3] Smooth the decorative paper over the first chipboard section and then spread an even coat of glue over to the next section. You'll cover the chipboard sheet by gluing and smoothing one section at a time and using the edge of the table to make each fold crease as you go.

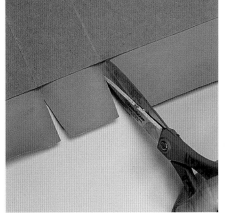

4] These creases are crucial to keep the cover paper from tearing as you fold the folio into place.

5] Flip the body over and cut darts into the cover paper at each fold point.

7] Cut the 8½" x 11" cardstock in half lengthwise. Use the pattern provided on page 61 to cut side gussets. Glue the tabs into place at the bottom fold and let dry completely before you move on to the next step.

6] Glue all the edges into place.

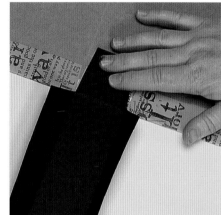

8] After the bottom flap is dry on the side gusset, glue the side tabs into place just inside the edge of the chipboard body. Pinch the top of the gusset together and use clips to hold the edges while they are drying. Remember to use scrap chipboard placed between the clips and the body to keep the clips from marring your project surface.

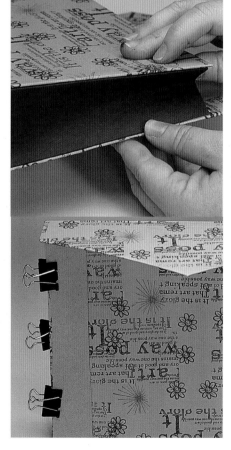

9] Trace the front flap onto a piece of 8½" x 11" text-weight paper. Cut this out for a liner.

10] Glue the liner into place. Use a stylus and a straightedge to make sure that the liner paper is glued down and creased nicely at the folds.

11] This is an optional step: I used photographic tape to apply an attractive black edge to the entire folio and a crisscross design on the front flap.

12] Attach a decorative medallion to the front flap and a magnet for the closure.

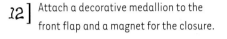

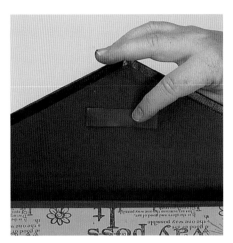

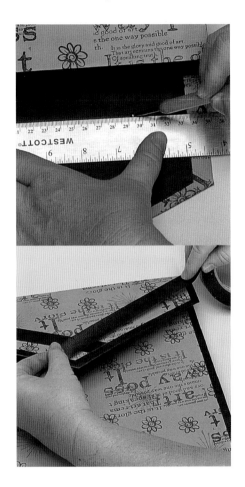

Variation

Stamping on kraft paper and then drawing over the whole design with a gold Krylon marker results in this decorative paper cover. Note the use of beads for embellishment. I used a magnet for closure on this project as well.

PATTERN FOR A POCKET FOLIO

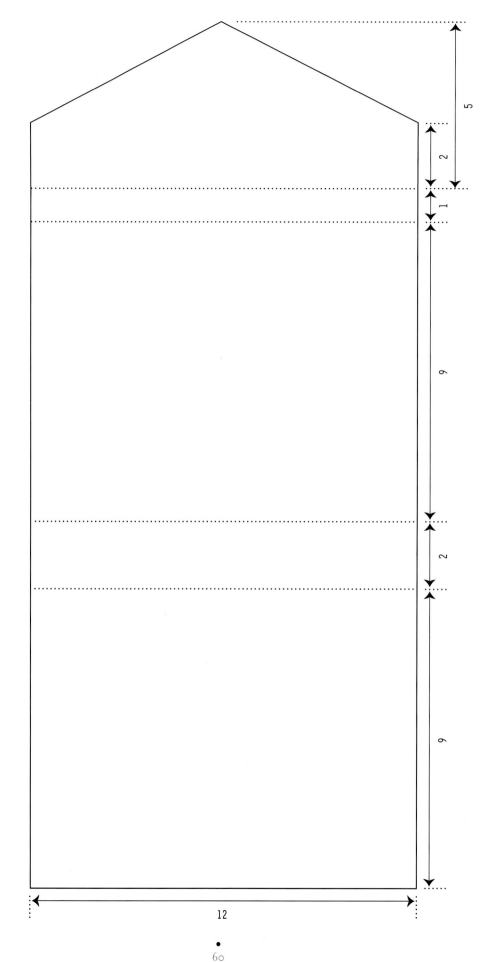

5

2

1

9

2

9

12

PATTERN FOR THE SIDE GUSSETS ON THE POCKET FOLIO

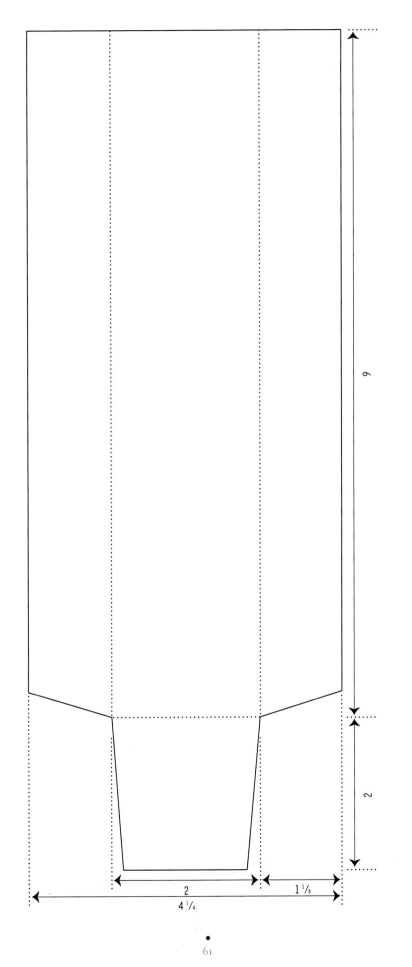

shadow box

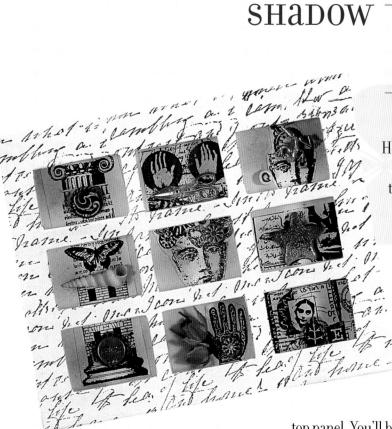

Here is a shadow box that is equally at home sitting on an easel or hanging on a wall. It is also great used as a top for a box or an artist's book assemblage. Made in a smaller version, it can be a necklace or pin. Again, don't let the complicated look fool you. This project is based on a simple box pattern with a cutout top panel. You'll be amazed at how easy it is to make.

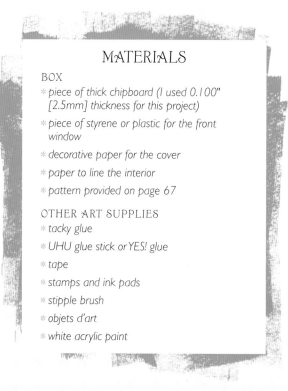

MATERIALS

BOX
* piece of thick chipboard (I used 0.100"
  [2.5mm] thickness for this project)
* piece of styrene or plastic for the front
  window
* decorative paper for the cover
* paper to line the interior
* pattern provided on page 67

OTHER ART SUPPLIES
* tacky glue
* UHU glue stick or YES! glue
* tape
* stamps and ink pads
* stipple brush
* objets d'art
* white acrylic paint

1] Transfer the measurements of the shadow box pattern to the chipboard, and cut out all the pieces: one top panel with the windows cut out, one bottom panel, one inner box piece, two short sides, two long sides, two short cross pieces and two long cross pieces. Use a stylus to score one side of the inner box piece, then flip it over and use the knife to score the other side along the dotted lines. Fold the sides up with the knife score on the outside edge.

2] Use the tape to secure the corners on the box piece.

3] Note that the folded outside edge is the edge that has been scored with the knife.

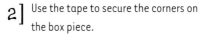

4] Spread glue over the bottom of the box and cover it with paper.

5] Make a crease along the edges to facilitate a nice turn of the paper as shown.

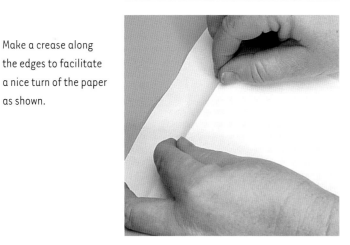

6] Clip darts out of the corners of the paper as shown, leaving tabs on the long edges.

7] Glue the long, tabbed edges in first, then glue the endpapers into place to cover the box.

8] Cut a piece of paper to line the inside bottom of the box, if you like.

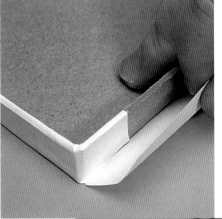

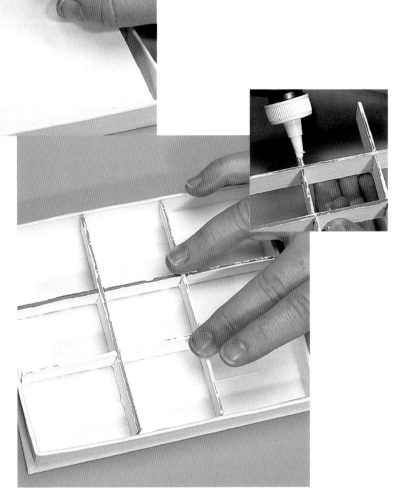

9] Cover the bottom panel with paper and glue it to the backside of the box assembly. Use tacky glue or YES! glue for this step.

10] Paint the cross strips with white acrylic paint and let them dry. Assemble all four pieces by interlocking them together. Put tacky glue on the ends and place them down into the box section, holding them in place until the glue starts to set. Then let the assembly dry.

11] Stamp and color your images with the stipple brush. Fill the box sections with cool stuff.

12] Cut the styrene to fit into the box section, and use tacky glue to secure it to the crossed support assembly.

13] Cut the window frame following the pattern measurements.

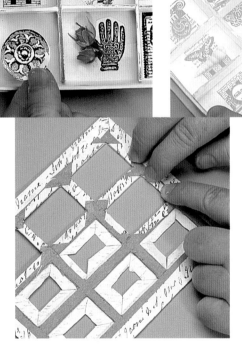

14] Cover the frame with decorative paper. This paper has been stamped with an Acey Deucy text stamp.

15] Put tacky glue on the back of the frame and lay it over the top piece, holding it in place until the glue begins to set.

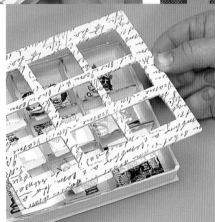

➡➡ THIS *box was created using a large text stamp from Stampers Anonymous and small seashells for the interior decoration. The decorative paper for the cover was done with marbling inks.*

➡➡ THIS *version has a frame that has an image stamped over white acrylic paint. Notice how the black ink was absorbed by the acrylic paint, turning the stamped image to a gray color. This effect is not unattractive, but you should be aware of it, in case you want a solid black.*

⬆ HERE *is a mini version of a single-paned shadow box. It made an adorable pin.*

PATTERN FOR SHADOW BOX

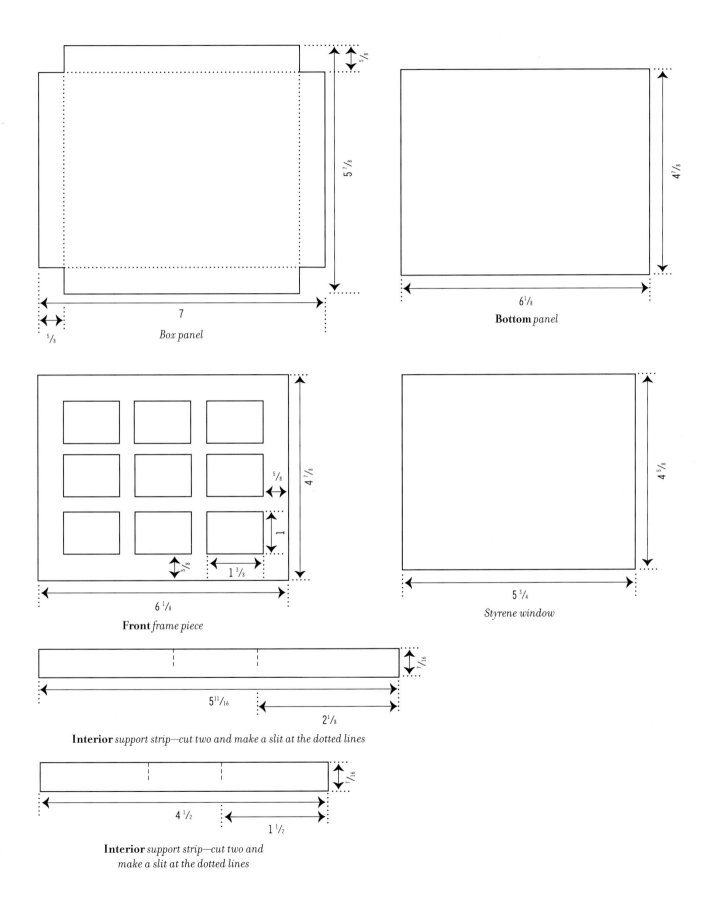

$5/8$

$5\frac{7}{8}$

7

$5/8$

Box panel

$4\frac{7}{8}$

$6\frac{1}{8}$

Bottom *panel*

$5/8$

$4\frac{7}{8}$

1

$5/8$

$1\frac{3}{8}$

$6\frac{1}{8}$

Front *frame piece*

$4\frac{5}{8}$

$5\frac{3}{4}$

Styrene window

$7/16$

$5\frac{11}{16}$

$2\frac{1}{8}$

Interior *support strip—cut two and make a slit at the dotted lines*

$7/16$

$4\frac{1}{2}$

$1\frac{1}{2}$

Interior *support strip—cut two and
make a slit at the dotted lines*

pendant
purse

This purse is simply stunning, with a richness in texture and color

that is surprisingly easy to create. As with all the art in this book, the

results of your efforts will be unique and rewarding. This is a great

project where you can happily use those beautiful papers that you've been

collecting for a special, one-of-a-kind heirloom-quality gift.

MATERIALS

PURSE
* *thin chipboard (I used 0.050" [1.3mm] thickness for this project.)*
* *decorative paper for the cover*
* *pattern on page 73*
* *braided fabric or paper trim*
* *1 ½ yard of cord*
* *four brass ¼" (6mm) eyelets and setter*
* *large bead and end caps*

OTHER ART SUPPLIES
* *tacky glue*
* *Krylon Crystal Clear spray*
* *UHU glue stick or YES! glue*
* *¼" (6mm) paper punch*

1] Transfer the dimensions of the oval purse pattern (page 73) onto your chipboard and cut out the pieces or use a template to choose an oval of a size that you like. Note that you will need a slightly larger oval for the purse top than for the bottom.

2] The top and the body of the purse are made in exactly the same manner, with the top being a little larger in order to fit over the bottom section. Preshape the oval sides by forming them into a slight curve. Glue the paper to the outside of the curved paper for the exterior sides of the purse. Glue the paper to the inside of the curve on the interior side of the chipboard strip.

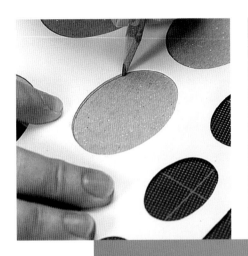

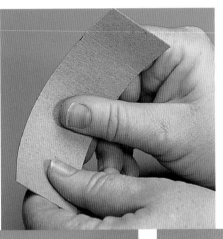

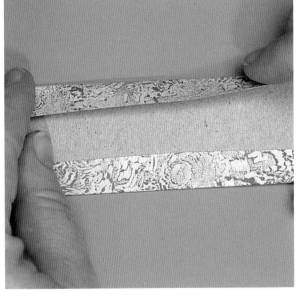

3] Glue the edges over and down.

4] Shape the sides of the top and body of the purse as you glue the papers on them. Fold the ends over and glue them down.

5] Cut a piece of paper a little larger than the chipboard oval and glue it down as shown. Clip the edges and glue them one at a time for a smooth cover.

6] Cut a liner piece of paper a tiny bit smaller than the oval, and glue it into place as shown.

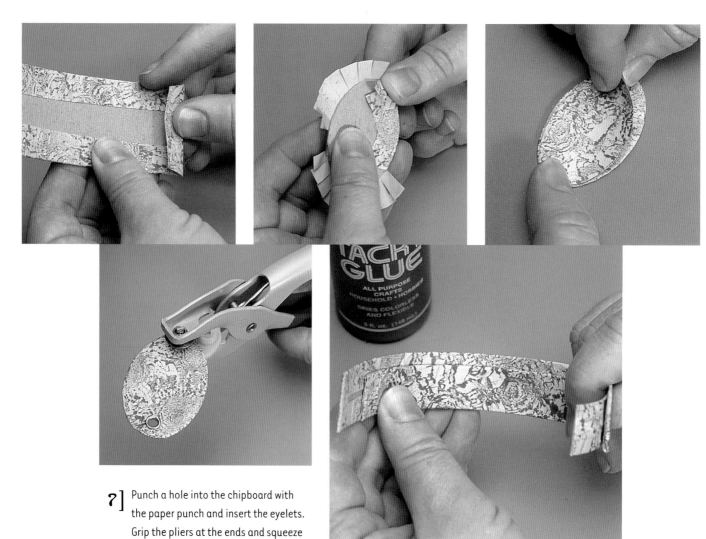

7] Punch a hole into the chipboard with the paper punch and insert the eyelets. Grip the pliers at the ends and squeeze tightly to secure the eyelets.

8] Use tacky glue to join the side strips together. Note that you will want to stagger the ends of the strips and make a little niche into which both pieces will settle.

10] Place a bead of glue around the rim niche and glue the oval piece into place. Do the same for both the top and base of the purse.

9] Hold the edges down until the glue sets.

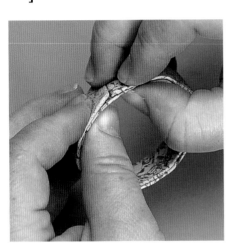

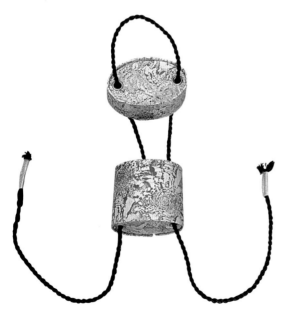

12] Thread a bead cap, a large bead and the second cap onto the cords.

11] Thread the cord through both pieces of the purse as shown. Note that you will need a much longer cord for a strap than I've used in the step-by step-pictures. I just didn't have a piece of cord long enough at the time.

13] Attach the tassel to the end cord low enough for the large bead to slide over and cover the attachment knot.

14] Slide the beads down over the tassel knot and secure them with tacky glue.

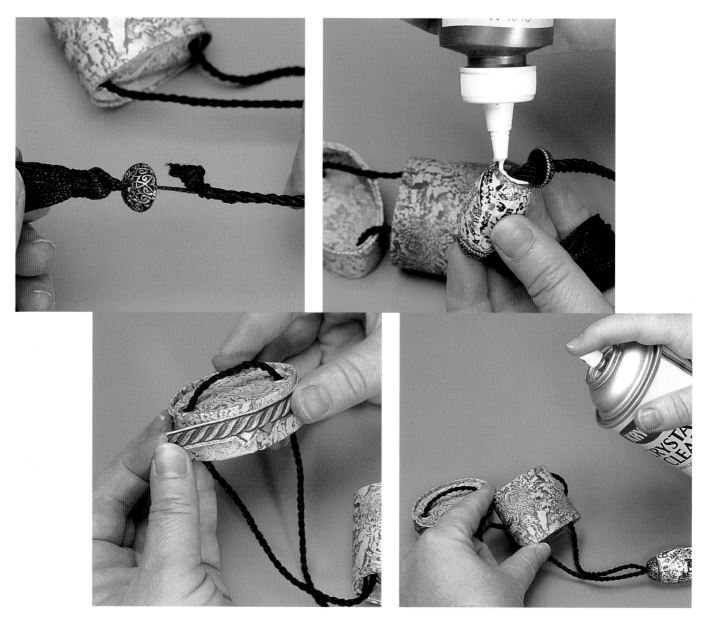

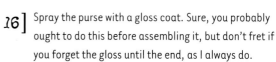

15] Add paper or fabric trim wherever you like. Use the tacky glue to secure it in place.

16] Spray the purse with a gloss coat. Sure, you probably ought to do this before assembling it, but don't fret if you forget the gloss until the end, as I always do.

PATTERN FOR OVAL PURSE PENDANT

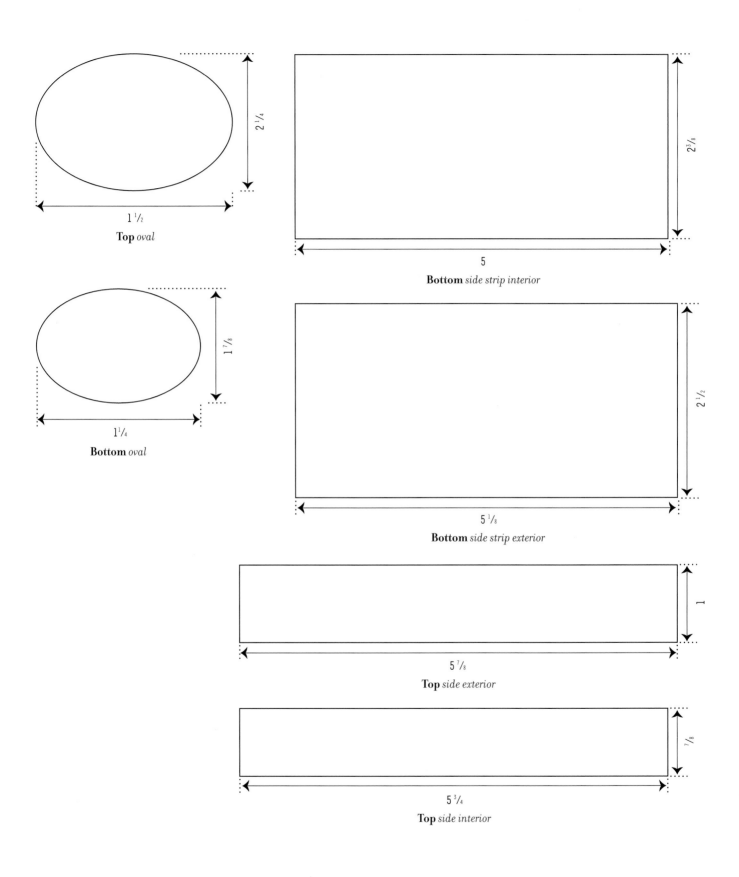

Top *oval*

2 1/4

1 1/2

Bottom *oval*

1 7/8

1 1/4

Bottom *side strip interior*

2 3/8

5

Bottom *side strip exterior*

2 1/2

5 1/8

Top *side exterior*

1

5 7/8

Top *side interior*

7/8

5 3/4

BURNISHED METAL
Container

With a few simple tools, you can make an

ordinary tin container into an extraordi-

nary treasure box. There are few things

as beautiful and captivating as the swirls

of iridescent blue, black and green pati-

nas that develop when you burn tin. You'll want

to make several of these gems for gifts, as well as for yourself.

MATERIALS

CONTAINER
* *tin container (I used an inexpensive brass-coated pillbox. If you find such a box that says it's from China, chances are it's made of tin with a very thin coat of brass that will burn off in the fire. That is the type of box you want for this project.)*

OTHER ART SUPPLIES
* *tongs or needle-nose pliers to hold the hot item*
* *stamps with bold images on them (I used a stamp from JudiKins)*
* *Ultra Thick Embossing Enamel or Amazing Glaze*
* *Silver Rub 'n Buff and Metallic Rub-ons*
* *a pad of clear embossing ink*
* *colored embossing powders*

1] Hold the tin box in a flame until the coating burns off and the swirls of iridescent color emerge. Remember to douse the hot tin in cool water before you touch it.

2] Pat the clear embossing ink all over the top of the container.

3] Emboss the top with a coat of Ultra-Thick Embossing Enamel or Amazing Glaze. While still hot, pour a second coat on the box top and heat to melt. Repeat for a third coat and while the powder is still hot, sprinkle other colors into it and heat to melt.

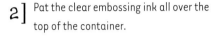

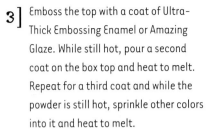

4] While the embossing powder is hot, press the stamp into it and hold it a second or two until the powder cools.

⬆ THIS *tin has been finished with clear powder and topped with silver Rub 'n Buff and Metallic Rub-ons. You can use a cloth to apply these products, but your fingers will give you better control over the application. The coloring products are oil-based and will take a day to cure. You may need to seal them with Krylon Crystal Clear if you need to use the box immediately.*

very VELVET
pouch

The time spent creating these lovely velvet pouches will not be

time wasted. Everyone can use a handsome and handcrafted

drawstring pouch to house his or her important treasures.

This gift can easily be tailored to your friends' tastes

and needs by making it larger or smaller, changing

the color and possibly even changing the drawstring

treatment to a corded purse handle for slinging across

a shoulder. Think about beading directly on the body of the

purse and possibly sewing contrasting strips of fabric and fancy fibers to it as well. The basic direc-

tions are given below, but try to visualize all the possibilities for this project as you read.

MATERIALS

VELVET POUCH
* two pieces of velvet cut ¼" (6mm) to ½" (12mm) larger than your finished project on all sides
* cord for the drawstring

OTHER ART SUPPLIES
* stamps with bold, simple images
* iron
* spray bottle filled with water
* fabric scissors

* needle and thread or sewing machine
* length of prestrung beads or assorted beads to string by hand
* brush markers
* paintbrush
* household bleach
* opaque and metallic gel roller pens
* safety pin
* Fray Check
* Scotch tape

Before beginning Any type of velvet will work for this project. Even velveteen will work, but of course the fabric finish will not be as luxurious as real velvet. All blends of velvet will burn at different iron settings. Pure silk velvet can take a higher heat and will make the cleanest impressions, whereas synthetic blends will melt at a much lower heat. Try your hot iron on scraps first. I usually buy an inexpensive blend of rayon and acetate velvet and set the iron at the beginning of the 4 setting, which is for cotton. When I'm ironing on silk velvet, I move the setting up to 5.

You can buy a sheet of Teflon ironing material at a fabric store, and it really helps to lay it over your test piece of velvet before touching the hot iron to it. That way if the iron is hot enough to melt the velvet, you won't get a gooey mess stuck to the bottom of your iron. (Trust me, you don't want to have to clean that off your iron.) If the velvet melts to your stamp, don't worry. Let it cool and then use a little pick to pick the melted velvet out of the stamp grooves. It will pop out fairly easily.

Also, avoid touching the part of the iron with the steam holes to the velvet. It will leave little round marks on your pattern. I touch the iron down on the front edge for a small stamp and at the center back for a large stamp to avoid those holes. Do not press back and forth or rock the iron while ironing the image. It will prevent a clean depression in the velvet. You must touch the iron straight down and hold it for a count of about six and then pull straight back up. No back-and-forth ironing action!

The high heat will not hurt the rubber stamps. Some cushions, such as the gray cushion found on some stamps, will melt after repeated use of a single stamp at a high temperature. I alleviate that problem by using multiple stamps, letting the hot ones cool a little before the next impression is made with them.

The last thing to note is that I used markers and gel rollers for fun and because I had them close at hand. If you are looking for a more colorfast option, then you'll definitely want to use dyes and fabric paints to color your velvet.

1] Cut your velvet to size, and mist it with water.

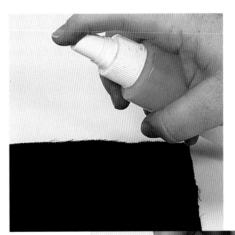

2] Lay the stamp onto your work surface facing up. Remember to choose stamps with bold, simple images. Place the velvet face down onto the stamp.

3] Press the hot iron onto the assembly and hold it for a count of about six seconds.

4] Here is a picture of a fully stamped piece of velvet. I used Hero Arts, Clearsnap and RubberStampede stamps for this project.

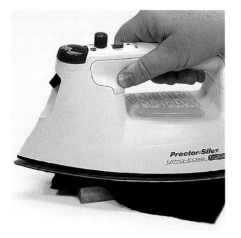

5] Pour a little household bleach into a small container and use a disposable synthetic brush to bleach the color out of the stamped images. At this point it should be noted that bleach is caustic, so create good ventilation in your workspace to avoid inhaling the fumes. The straight bleach will weaken the fabric slightly over time, so you will not want to use this bleaching method on items that will receive a lot of stress. For instance, a decorative pillow would be fine, but not a seat cushion or something that will be sat or lain upon. A vest would be fine, but not a jacket with pull on the sleeves. Get the picture? If you make a large purse that will hold heavy items, you'll definitely want to line the purse with a sturdy fabric. You must also caution the recipient of your gift that this item is to be drycleaned only. The good news is that if the color washes out, markers may be used to add the color back in. If you think colorfastness will be an issue, be sure to use fabric markers, dyes and paints for this project. After the bleach has done its duty, you can paint color back into the piece with brush markers and fabric markers. You can color directly on the fabric for a more intense look, or you can brush some water onto the areas first to allow color bleeds.

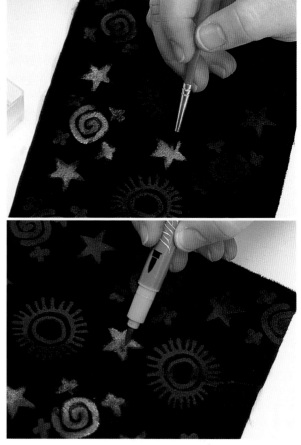

6] I also like to use the metallic and
opaque gel rollers to add detail to
the images.

7] After the fabric is dry, begin to assemble the pouch. Baste the beads onto the
bottom of the fabric as shown.

8] Place the backing fabric onto the front,
right sides together, and sew around
the three closed edges of the pouch,
keeping the beads to the inside.

9] Finish the open edge of the pouch with Fray Check. On a larger pouch, you may want to consider turning the edge of the casing in twice for a more finished look.

10] Fold the top edge down flat and sew all around to make a casing for the cord.

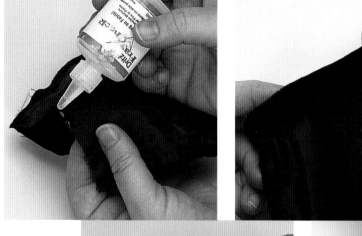

11] Turn the pouch right side out.

12] Put a dab of Fray Check at the place where the front opening for the cord will be cut. Let it dry completely.

13] Use sharp fabric scissors to carefully cut a small opening at the front center of the pouch casing, right where you painted the Fray Check.

14] Wrap a piece of tape around the end of your cord and cut it to a little point. Thread this onto a safety pin.

15] Here's a little secret: If you tuck the pointed end of the cord into the head of the safety pin, the whole assembly will slide through the casing much more easily.

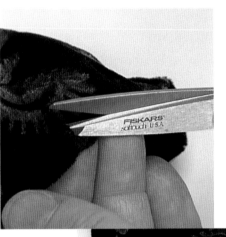

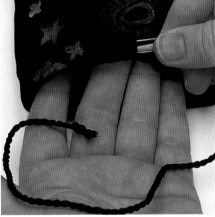

↑ YOU *can just tie the ends of the cord into knots if you like, or hang tassels or beads from it.*

fabric
pins

Always excellent conversation pieces, these pins are a great project

that you can make as simple or as complex as you like. All the pins

start with the basic techniques shown in this project, and then they

are treated to extra special touches, including beads, dimensional

fabric paint and assorted backing boards.

MATERIALS

FABRIC PINS
* natural muslin (enough for the fronts and backs of your pins)
* stuffing material
* optional embellishments—assorted beads, metallic fibers, charms and interesting mounting boards
* pin back

OTHER ART SUPPLIES
* stamps
* skewer for the stuffing
* needle and black thread or a sewing machine threaded with black thread
* assorted fabric paints and paintbrushes
* a black Fabrico inkpad
* Fray Check
* black permanent ink pen
* tacky glue

1] Stamp your image in black Fabrico ink. This picture shows an Acey Deucy un-mounted stamp attached to an acrylic HALOS system block using hook-and-loop strips. Use your heat gun to set the ink, readying it for watercolors.

2] Paint the image with fabric paints. To avoid obscuring the stamped lines, you may need to thin some types of paints a little. Createx and Ready Tex are sheer enough to let the stamped lines show through, but Polymark and Tulip paints will need thinning with water.

3] Use a wide brush to paint coordinating fabric paints on the fabric for the back side of the pin. Pictured is an application of lavender and orange fabric paint. The next color added is a gold metallic fabric paint. Use your heat gun to speed the drying process.

5] Use a smaller paintbrush to color the stamped images with fabric paint.

4] Stamp an all-over pattern in black Fabrico ink and set with a heat gun.

6] Choose a spot on the decorative backing fabric and position the front piece over it, so that the decorated sides of both pieces of fabric face outward. Sew the two pieces together with tiny stitches. With the right side of both pieces facing outward, you won't have to turn these pins right side out after sewing.

7] You may want to use a black permanent ink pen to color in the lines that may have been covered with paint. I used a micro Uniball Vision pen from an office supply store. You need to choose a pen that will be both waterproof and bleed-proof on the fabric.

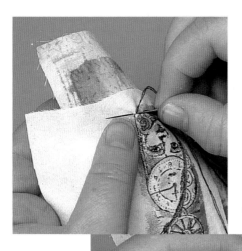

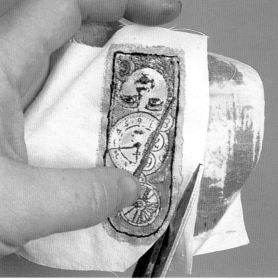
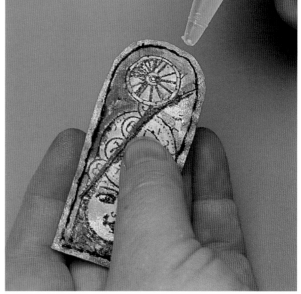

8] Use a sharp pair of scissors to cut out the pin, leaving about a 1/8" (3mm) margin all around the sewn edge. The pin can remain as it is, or you can embellish it further with beads, fibers and charms.

9] Use Fray Check on the raw edges to prevent raveling of the fabric. Let it dry naturally, or use a heat gun to hurry the drying process along.

10] Pinch the pin so that the back side will come up to make it easy to cut a slit for the filling.

11] Use a skewer to push tiny amounts of filler into the pin until it is filled to a nice level.

12] Use white tacky glue to affix a little patch of fabric over the filler opening. Sew or glue a small pinback to your project.

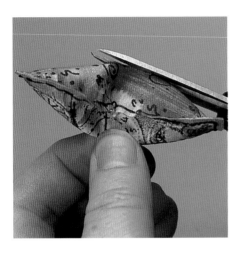

➤→
THIS *little pin has also been stamped with an ERA Graphics image. The basic piece was then embellished with beads and metallic thread. The headdress is one-half of a brass-colored hanger from a Christmas tree bulb. You can flatten them out and burn them to get rid of the brass color, creating an interesting, "aged" patina.*

←◄
THIS *pin has been stamped twice with an image from ERA Graphics. The second image was cut out to reveal only the flower portion. The flower was treated to the same techniques as the main pin and then attached with tacky glue. A decorative button was glued onto the flower. Colored beads were added to the overall piece by using Polymark dimensional fabric paint. A beaded ornament was attached to the bottom of the pin with a gold jump ring.*

envirotex
pins

Here is a pin that always gets the comment,

"That's done with rubber stamps? No way!"

This is another simple but sophisticated

method of producing very sellable merchan-

dise. Your customers will snap multiples of

them up for gifts as well as for themselves.

EnviroTex Lite can be used to make pins, neck-

laces, bracelets, charms and medallions for your books and boxes. There are lots and lots of uses for

this particular project so go ahead, have fun and know that you are producing a valuable and lovely

piece of artwork.

MATERIALS

PIN
* *EnviroTex Lite or any brand of resin*
* *chipboard for the back of the pin*
* *black cardstock*
* *pinback*

OTHER ART SUPPLIES
* *stamps (I used a stamp from ERA Graphics)*
* *plastic measuring cup*
* *craft stick or stirring tool*
* *push pins and a piece of foamcore*
* *poster tack putty*
* *colored pencils, including white*
* *embossing ink and gold embossing powder*
* *black felt-tip pen*
* *glue stick and tacky glue*

1] Stamp an image in embossing ink on
black paper and emboss with gold
embossing powder. Use a sharp white
colored pencil to color a base coat. Try
to avoid running into the embossing
with your pencil because it could nick
off the embossing powder. After you've
laid down your basecoat of white, color
over it with the colors of your choice.
The white undercoat will make the
colored pencil show up much better on
the black paper.

2] Glue the colored image onto the piece
of chipboard with a glue stick.

3] Coat the edges with embossing ink.

4] Pour a little pile of gold embossing
powder onto a scrap piece of paper and
dip the edges of the pin into it.

5] Emboss the edges, making sure not to
aim the gun at your fingers.

6] Stick the push pin into the foamcore and put a little ball of poster tack putty on top of the pin. Place the project piece onto the poster tack securely in as level a manner as you can. Larger pieces will require three tacks to stand evenly.

❦ HERE *are two pins on their stands ready for the EnviroTex. Note that the projects are on raised pins so that you can use a wrapped finger or a craft stick to wipe off drips that may form under the project.*

7] Pour a small amount of resin (try to mix only what you will use) into a mixing cup and then add an equal amount of catalyst. Mix well for about two minutes. If you do not mix equal parts resin and catalyst, or you don't mix them well, you will have a mess that dries sticky to the touch.

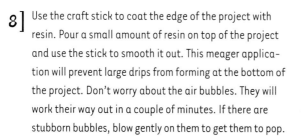

9] After the resin has dried overnight, use a utility knife to carefully dig just beneath the surface of the chipboard to remove any drips. Don't try to cut through the resin with your knife.

8] Use the craft stick to coat the edge of the project with resin. Pour a small amount of resin on top of the project and use the stick to smooth it out. This meager application will prevent large drips from forming at the bottom of the project. Don't worry about the air bubbles. They will work their way out in a couple of minutes. If there are stubborn bubbles, blow gently on them to get them to pop.

11] Cut a piece of black backing cardstock (leather and felt work great as backings, too) and lay the pinback down to measure for the opening.

12] Cut a tiny T shape so that you can insert the ends of the pinback into the liner as shown.

10] Use a felt-tip pen to color the back edges of the chipboard.

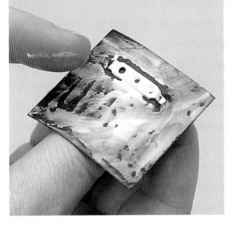

13] Use tacky glue to coat the back side of the liner.

14] Place the liner and pinback on the back of your project and press down to secure them.

Clay Works

MOST CLAYS LEND THEM-
SELVES BEAUTIFULLY TO
RUBBER STAMPING.
WHAT BETTER WAY TO
MAKE AN IMPRESSION
THAN INTO A SOFT, MAL-
LEABLE MATERIAL?

I USE TWO TYPES OF
CLAY EXTENSIVELY:
PAPERCLAY AND POLYMER
CLAY. BOTH ARE INEX-
PENSIVE AND READILY
AVAILABLE, AND REQUIRE
MINIMUM EXPERTISE TO
CREATE LOVELY LITTLE
TREASURES WORTHY OF
HEIRLOOM STATUS.

Paperclay basics *

For our purposes, you can think of paperclay as nothing more than thick, wet paper. Paperclay dries to a light weight, making it ideal for projects such as jewelry, card embellishments, vessels, sculpture and much more.

I use Creative Paperclay. It is ready to use with no type of conditioning required. There is an expiration date on the package, so be sure to check that before buying. Even if the clay has not expired, feel the package to make sure it is not too hard. If, by the time you use your clay, it has hardened a little, hydrate it by breaking it into smaller chunks, putting them into a self-sealing plastic bag and adding a couple tablespoons of water. Leave it a day or two until the clay has absorbed the water. When you take it out of the bag, work it with your hands into an even consistency.

Color can be added to the wet clay with any type of pigment. Try acrylic paint or dyes and pigment inks that you use to re-ink your stamp pads. Just squeeze in a little and work it through with your hands. Remember that too much paint may make the clay too wet and unusable, so be a little sparing here. The clay will dry to a lighter shade than you see in the wet version.

One tip: It is a very absorbent paper, so a heavy coat of watercolor, for instance, will soften the piece, and you will have to allow for additional drying time before completion.

You can roll your clay out on a smooth surface with a drinking glass or a rolling pin. I use a piece of PVC pipe as my rolling pin. You can also flatten the clay with your hands. The thicker the clay, the longer the drying time, so keep that in mind for your projects.

You can air-dry or bake the clay. If you air-dry it, set it on a cooling sheet or a screen of some type so that it can dry equally on both sides. If not, the clay will curl upward as it dries (turn it over if you see this happening).

If you are impatient, you can oven-bake your clay. If you bake it on a cookie sheet, remember to check every 15 minutes or so for that curl, then turn the piece over so the other side can have a chance at drying. Repeat as often as necessary. The temperature should be about 225°F (107°C) and will take about 30 minutes for each 1/4" (6mm) of thickness. If you can set the piece on a screen, it will dry flatter and quicker. Warping will occur occasionally due to uneven drying, but don't let that upset you. Remember that this is just thick paper, so to cure this problem you can dunk your clay piece in water, take it out and wait a couple of seconds for the paper to absorb the water; then gently push it back into shape and start the drying process over again.

The dried clay will break if it is dropped, bent or mutilated. Still, it is a surprisingly durable once it is coated with a finish. If you should accidentally crack a piece of dried clay, use white glue to mend it. Once you've completed the finishing process, the repair won't show at all.

If you need to put a finish on the clay, and you have an absorption or a bleeding problem, think about sealing the dried piece of clay with a coat of white glue, gesso or a sealing spray. After you let this dry, you should be able to add the finish with less bleeding. If your chosen medium beads up on the sealant, try spraying the piece with a coat of workable fixative.

One last thing: You may stamp an impression into wet clay with an uninked stamp, or you may want to stamp into it with ink for a colored image. This is wet paper, so any dye or watercolor ink will run when it comes into contact with the clay. Use a pigment ink, the kind used for inking your embossing pads, for the best results. Also, remember that you must not press too hard with an inked stamp, or the ink will smudge.

Polymer clay basics *

Polymer clay is heavier than paper clay, so you may want to consider using only very small amounts to embellish cards and other paper products.

Unlike paper clay, polymer clay has to be conditioned before use. To condition the clay, simply roll it between your hands until a rope is formed. Fold the rope over, twist it, then fold over and twist again. Roll this out to another smooth rope and repeat the process three or four times. The clay should now be softened, conditioned and ready for use. Colors can be blended in the same manner.

I prefer to use Premo! clay, a product of Sculpey, for my stamp art projects. It is slightly flexible after baking, which makes it very durable for pins and other wearable art. There is no right or wrong polymer clay, though. Try several brands and learn their individual properties before deciding which clay is the best for your project.

You can roll out polymer clay on a smooth surface with a glass or an acrylic brayer. A piece of cellophane or deli wrap under your clay works well as a work surface.

Unlike paper clay, polymer clay must be baked. Ideally, use a toaster oven that is devoted to crafts to bake your clay. Follow the manufacturer's directions on each pack of clay for exact baking time and tempera-

ture. Notice that the directions on the packages are for pieces 1/4" (6mm) thick, so if you've rolled out a thinner piece you must lower the temperature and the cooking time a little. I usually lower the oven 15–20°F (8–11°C) and knock five minutes off the baking time, which seems to work well.

Once your clay has cured, you can use a fine-grit wet-dry sandpaper to smooth the edges if necessary. You can get a really nice shine on your clay piece by graduating down to an ultrafine 600-grit paper and then using a soft cloth or muslin buffing wheel.

You can also use finishes made for polymer clay or a waterbased product. Acrylics work very well on polymer clay. Some lacquers, such as nail polish, will react with the polymer clay and leave you with a sticky-gooey mess that will never dry.

The last thing you need to know about polymer clay basics is that unbaked clay can meld with some plastic storage containers. To check your container, put a little piece of clay on the plastic. Wait ten minutes and see if the clay comes off cleanly or if a meld begins. I store my uncured clay in plastic bags with no problems.

Here is an amulet that was made by thoroughly mixing Scenic Sand into translucent polymer clay to get the green colors. The clay was rolled out, cut into shape and baked. The cured clay was then buffed to a nice shine, and two scrap pieces of shrink art were glued to the front of it. This is a variation on the Poly Dolly necklace project.

PAPERCLAY
medallion

This paperclay medallion can be used as a pin or a
pendant for a necklace. It's also lightweight
enough that it works great as an embellishment for cards, boxes or books. Paperclay
can be fragile so you may want to back your
piece with a thin sheet of chipboard cut
and colored to blend with the finished art piece.

MATERIALS

MEDALLION
* paperclay

OTHER ART SUPPLIES
* stamps
* deli wrap paper
* a clay roller, such as a PVC pipe
* fine sandpaper
* craft knife
* black acrylic paint
* Metallic Rub-ons and Rub 'n Buff in assorted
  colors
* clear and colored embossing inks
* Ultra Thick Embossing Enamel or Amazing
  Glaze
* Treasure Crystal Cote glaze (optional)
* Krylon Gold Leafing pen

2] Use an uninked stamp to press an image into the clay. For this piece, I used a heart stamp by Love You to Bits. My stamp looks like it has ink on it (from stains), but it really is uninked—honest.

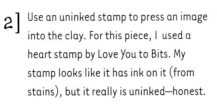

1] Lay your clay on the deli wrap and use the PVC pipe to roll it out to about $1/8$" (3mm) to $1/4$" (6mm) in thickness.

3] Use a knife to cut the paper clay piece out and allow to dry.

4] After the clay is dry, sand the edges to make them smooth.

5] Paint a coat of black acrylic paint over the piece and let it dry.

6] Use Metallic Rub-ons or Rub 'n Buff to apply color to the surface of the heart.

7] Use the gold pen to add extra shine to the outlines of the heart.

8] Coat the finished clay piece with Crystal Cote glaze or some other type of sealant.

THIS is the completed medallion. To finish, drill a hole into the clay heart with a pin vise and attach it to a corded necklace with a brass jump ring.

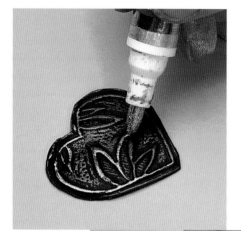

9] The next photos show a slightly different way to finish the pin. The heart stamp is by Moe Wubba. The baked, plain white clay is tapped lightly with different colors of embossing ink. Keep the impressed lines free of ink to keep the white color.

10] Pour Amazing Glaze or Ultra Thick Embossing Enamel onto the clay and tap off the excess.

←

THIS *pin was done in the same way as the clay heart, only the hand (an Acey Deucy stamp) was layered onto a larger piece of clay that had been stamped with a swirl stamp from All Night Media and then torn after baking to get that jagged edge.*

11] Heat the powder with your heat gun. While the embossing powder is still warm, put another coat of embossing powder on it, tap off the excess and re-heat it. Do this for three or four coats to create a very shiny, thick coat on the final piece.

12] Here is the finished clay medallion. Note that the shiny glaze sticks only to the inked part of the stamp, leaving the impressed lines looking like grout in an Italian tile.

←

THIS *pin was done in the same manner as the other two, but while the clay was wet, a trowel was pushed into the top and bottom edges and pulled away so that it made these cool little square points. This image is from a stamp by Too Much Fun. The painted pin was coated with Krylon Crystal Clear spray.*

←

THIS *sun pin is another example of this technique.*

➤➤ THIS *sun was painted with watercolors for a very vibrant look, then coated with clear embossing ink and treated to three coats of Ultra Thick Embossing Enamel.*

➤➤ THIS *pin was put together with pieces of old jewelry glued to a piece of chipboard that had been covered with thin copper metal. The clay itself was "aged" with acrylic paints.*

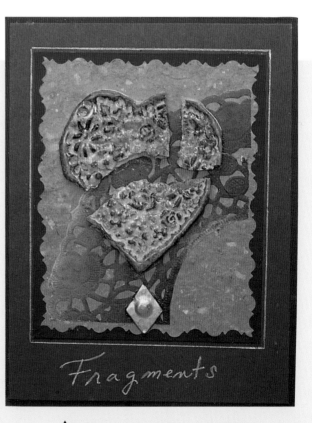

Fragments

↑ PAPERCLAY *is excellent for embellishing cards because it is lightweight. This heart (a PSX stamp) is watercolored and embossed.*

←◄

IMPRESS ME *makes a wonderful line of stamps that are great for making primitive pins. This pin has been painted with black acrylic paint and then colored with copper Metallic Rub-ons. Use a pin vise or a push pin to make small holes in which to thread beaded wires. Secure the wire ends on the back with a piece of book tape. Cover the back side of the pin in the same manner used to cover the back side of the EnviroTex pin to hide the tape and wire ends.*

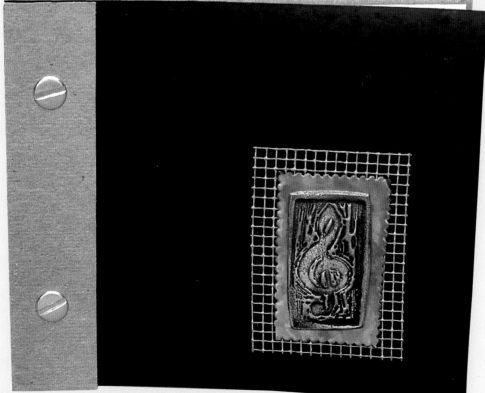

←◄

THIS *book, similar to the one on page 34, has a paperclay medallion on it.*

POLY DOLLY
necklace

A fun project for all ages, this little lady can be as simple or as intensely artsy as you care to make her. There are lots of options for stamping and embellishing her and her skirt. I've used Metallic Rub-ons for her bodice but acrylic paint also works beautifully with polymer clay. Think about other things to add such as coiled wire and fiber for hair, beads for bracelets and a necklace for her outfit and maybe even teeny little buttons too!

MATERIALS

NECKLACE
* half a block of polymer clay
* provided doll pattern (page 101)
* plastic doll hands (found in the dollmaking section of craft stores)
* ¼" (6mm) dowel cut down to arm size, with a screw eyelet screwed into the top ends
* cutout picture of a Victorian girl's face
* clear glass "gem" found in the floral department of craft stores
* two medium-size jump rings and two larger jump rings
* cord for necklace
* scrap leather for the backing and connection to the cord
* a "jewel" for her dress (if you like)
* thin chipboard for the skirt and materials to decorate it (you can use paint, stamps and/or papers)

* two ¼" (6mm) eyelets and a hammer
* two screw eyes (about ½" [12mm] long and ⅛" [3mm] in diameter)

OTHER ART SUPPLIES
* clay roller of some sort
* rubber stamps for texture
* Quick Grab glue or Zap-A-Gap
* white glue
* pin vise with a small drill bit
* deli wrap paper
* ¼" (6mm) hole punch
* craft knife
* acrylic craft paints
* Metallic Rub-ons

1] Cut the plastic arms off to resemble elbow-length opera gloves. Screw the eyelet into the top portion of the sanded dowel. Glue the other end of the wooden dowel into the doll's gloves.

2] Lay the conditioned clay on the deli wrap and roll it out to about ⅛" (3mm) in thickness.

3] Lay the paper pattern of the doll's torso on the clay and use the knife to cut around the pattern.

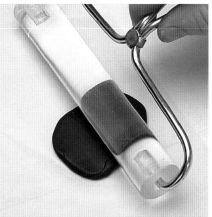

4] Use a rubber stamp to make a decorative impression in the clay. I used a stamp by Claudia Rose in this example.

5] Use white glue to fix the face in place, and then run a thin line of white glue around the floral "gem" and press it over the picture and into the clay. The white glue will dry clear when baked on the clay.

6] Contour the clay in a little to capture the "gem" face. You can make little designs around her bonnet, or you can even add hair and other clay decorations at this point. Bake the clay.

7] After the clay has been baked and cooled, apply Metallic Rub-ons to the raised surface of the doll's stamped torso.

8] Use a pin vise or a drill to drill holes for the jump rings to attach the arms and skirt.

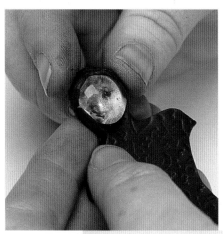  

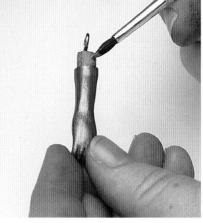 

9] Paint the arms and gloves with acrylic paints.

10] Use the skirt pattern to cut out a thin piece of chipboard, then decorate it with scraps of paper, beads, etc. Punch two holes with the hole punch and insert eyelets as shown. Use a tap of the hammer on the back side of the eyelets for a quick setting.

THIS *pin was made of black polymer clay that was stamped with a brick wall stamp (Gains & Mc-Call) and then brushed with Pearl Ex iridescent powders before baking. The little silver square is a piece of chipboard that has been embossed three times with Ultra Thick Embossing Enamel and silver embossing powder that was added onto the last layer of embossing. An uninked stamp (JudiKins) was impressed into the hot embossing powder to make the raised image.*

11] Thread the larger jump rings onto the bottom of the torso, and flatten them into an oval shape so the dolly will hang flat. Position the jump ring openings at the back center so that nothing will slip out of the rings. Attach the arms with the smaller jump rings.

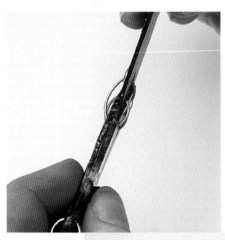

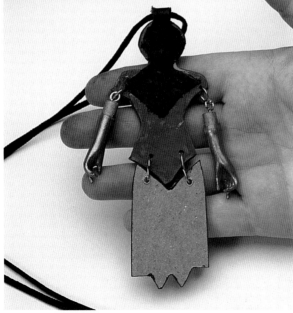

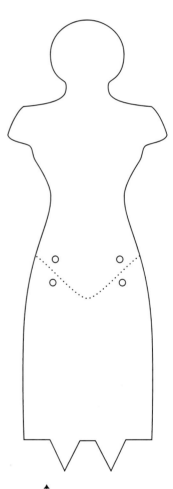

↑ PATTERN FOR POLY DOLLY NECKLACE

Cut out the pattern and cut it apart at the skirt/torso joint. Trace the skirt pattern onto thin chipboard and decorate the skirt as you wish. Lay the torso pattern on your slab of clay and cut around it with a craft knife.

12] You can make an attachment piece for the cord by cutting the leather roughly the shape of the doll with a long strip on top. Fold the strip down over the cord and glue it to the inside of the liner, between the leather liner and the polymer clay. Use Quick Grab to glue the entire assembly to the doll's back side. A folded piece of ribbon also works just fine as an attachment.

WINDOW *to* My art

These adorable mini shadow boxes make interesting pins and amulets as well as little works of art to hang on your wall or to brighten your desk. The frame housing a collage without the foamcore looks great on boxes, books and cards, too!

MATERIALS

WINDOW
* two pieces of chipboard cut to 2¼" x 3" (5.7cm x 7.6cm)
* styrene cut to 2¼" x 3" (5.7cm x 7.6cm)
* black ¼" (6mm) foamcore cut to 2¼" x 3" (5.7cm x 7.6cm) with a frame opening cut out so that the frame edge is just a little smaller than ¼" (6mm)
* a piece of tooling metal cut to about 2¾" x 3½" (6.4cm x 8.9cm)

OTHER ART SUPPLIES
* markers for writing on slick surfaces
* stamped images for collage
* stipple brush and dye inkpads
* colored pencils
* black felt tip pen
* Quick Grab glue
* assorted gewgaws for collage
* tweezers

1] Measure and cut out the center of one of the pieces of chipboard to make a frame that is ¼" (6mm) wide on all sides. Center the frame on the piece of metal and, using a utility cutter, cut an X in the center from inside corner to corner of the chipboard frame piece. Trim and fold up the inside edges to the back side of the frame piece.

2] Sandwich the styrene next to the frame piece and fold the metal edges up and over it to hold the plastic securely in place.

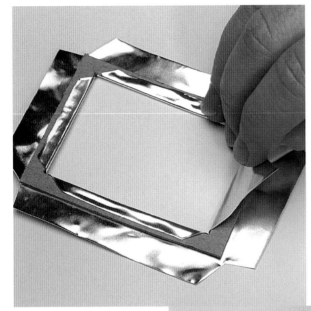

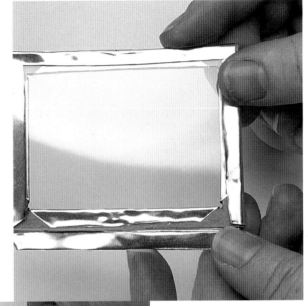

3] Use a stylus or any pointed tool to scribe designs into the front of the metal frame. You want your creation to have the charm of a handcrafted item, so don't worry about imperfection of line or tracing a pattern or anything. I let the pattern emerge as I work on the metal.

4] Use a marker for slick surfaces and a paper towel to brush on and rub off color until you get the desired effect.

5] I added a gold Marvy metallic marker to the previous layer of orange Design marker.

6] Collect all kinds of trinkets and paraphernalia for your shadow boxes, and don't worry about the strange or brassy colors. You can use markers or paints to color them.

7] Assemble the collage on top of the uncut piece of chip-board for your back piece. I glued a piece of paste paper to the chipboard before I applied the collage elements to it. Use a glue stick for the paper elements and Quick Grab or tacky glue for the charms and leaves. Color your stamped images with a stipple brush and dye inkpads.

THIS *is a slightly more complicated piece that was made by cutting a piece of foamcore in the approximate shape of an angel and then gluing metal findings and tooled metal cuttings onto it. Look closely and you'll see the brassy metal caps from Christmas ornaments and a gaudy, cheap plastic Christmas ornament. See the ornate top and bottom section? That's the plastic ornament cut in half. The whole assembly was then aged with Instant Rust products. The framed shadow box was glued to the center of the assembly. The stamped lady is from American Art Stamp.*

8] Glue the foamcore frame onto the collaged piece of chipboard backing and then use Quick Grab or tacky glue to attach the metal front assembly to the foamcore frame. Use a black felt tip pen to color the edges of the backing chipboard to match the black foamcore.

LIGHT UP *your life*

lampshades

You can make extraordinary lampshades using stamp art

with minimal effort and a whole lot of fun and creativity.

This is another craft that is so simple that a child can do

it—and the results will be fabulous. My secret for this

project is that I buy ugly lampshades that have made

their way to the sale bins (and rightfully so). Then I tear off the

ugly paper print, which usually reveals a plain white heatproof

shade underneath—an excellent base for stamped papers!

MATERIALS

LAMP
* *lampshade*
* *finishing tape (I used black photographic tape in most of these projects, but a few have the shade paper folded over the wires for a self-finish. Cloth tape would work well, too.)*
* *fancy trim (optional)*
* *paper to stamp on (I used 60lb white drawing paper)*

OTHER ART SUPPLIES
* *dye inkpads, including a black waterproof inkpad*
* *gold Krylon leafing pen*
* *glue stick and tacky glue*

2] Start at one edge of your paper and roll the lampshade very carefully across the paper, depositing an inked line to follow for your pattern. If you want to make a self-edging, cut the paper a little larger than the pattern on both top and bottom. I usually add only about a ³⁄₈" (10mm) margin, which should be sufficient to turn the stamped paper under and cover the metal frame.

1] The easiest way that I know of to create a pattern for your lampshade is to color the edges, top and bottom, with a dye inkpad. OK, the very easiest way is to use the ugly paper shade that you pulled off the original sale lamp and trace around it, but if you don't have that cover, try the dye method. It works!

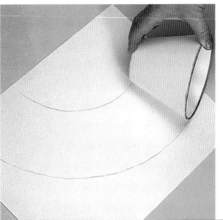

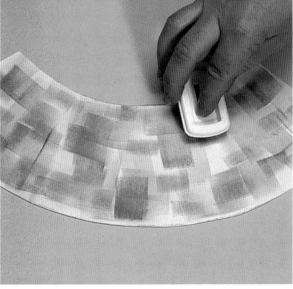

3] Use the dye inkpads to apply the ink colors directly to the paper by touching down and dragging them in alternate directions. The mini Vivid! ink pads from Clearsnap are perfect for this.

4] Add a little shine with the gold marker.

5] Use the splatter stamp from DeNami to apply another color.

6] Stamp random images in black ink. I'm using the Party People and Bubbles stamps by Claudia Rose.

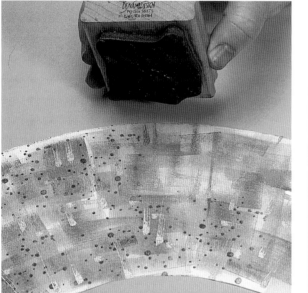

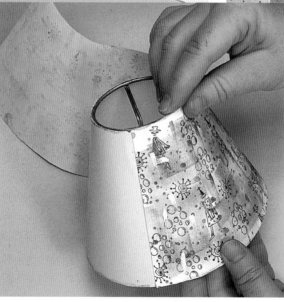

7] Use a glue stick to apply the paper to the lampshade. Remember, with glue sticks, you must get good and total coverage. Too little glue will make the project pop apart. Position the stamped paper on the shade and smooth it down.

8] Use the black tape as a finish, if you like. Again, ribbons and fabric work well, and so does cutting the paper with a ³⁄₈" (10mm) margin and folding that in for a self-finish.

↟ HERE'S *a shade self-finished by turning the margin under and over the frame wire. The decorative paper is colored brush markers scribbled over white tissue paper. The tissue was then laid on white art paper and spritzed with water so the color would bleed onto the white paper. I then stamped on a random pattern.*

◄ THIS *sophisticated shade was prepared with black stamping over white paper. Butterscotch-colored stars were added next. The gold-leafed swirls were easy, too. Just squirt a little leafing adhesive (found in craft stores) into a plastic dish. Spread it out to an even layer and ink your stamp with the adhesive. Stamp onto the shade paper, and let it dry. Remember to wash the adhesive off your stamp before it dries. After the adhesive dries to a tacky finish, apply gold leaf by laying it on the adhesive and brushing off the excess leaf.*

◄ THIS *shade was made by dragging the mini Vivid! dye inkpads across the paper, as in the first project sample. The bubbles (Claudia Rose) were stamped in black permanent ink and then colored with markers.*

9] Snip little cuts into the tape and fold it inward, smoothing out the overlaps and any crinkles you may make. Trim the inside tape with a knife, if necessary.

10] Use tacky glue to fix the trim into place.

beauTIFUL

beads

Beads have a wide variety of uses in the world of arts and crafts. The most obvious is jewelry, but you can also use your beads glued to the bottom of boxes for feet, glued to the top for handles, strung onto sling handles and in assemblage. Fancy fibers threaded through the large beads make wonderful tassels. Notice how pretty these stamped and decoupaged beads look on the cords of the oval purse projects.

MATERIALS

BEADS
* wooden beads of any size and shape

OTHER ART SUPPLIES
* fine-grit sandpaper
* paintbrush for use with glue
* stipple brush
* black waterproof inkpad
* straw-colored inkpad
* watercolors (optional)
* a sheet of white drawing paper
* Perfect Paper Adhesive
* colored pencils
* gloss coating (Crystal Cote makes a thick, shiny glaze, but plain old clear nail polish works well too.)

2] Stamp images in black waterproof ink and tear out. All of these images are from Acey Deucy.

3] Put a little Perfect Paper Adhesive (PPA) in a small container and dilute it with water so that it is like thick cream.

1] Sand the glossy finish off the bead.

4] Use the glue brush to apply a coat of PPA to the bead, then apply a coat of PPA to the back side of the paper.

5] Position the paper onto the bead and affix it with another coat of PPA on top of the paper.

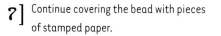
6] You can use the brush alone to smooth down the kinked paper for good adhesion, but I prefer to use my hands to really mold the paper to the curved surface of the bead. The PPA is not sticky at all—it feels like hand cream, so it's perfect for hands-on applications.

7] Continue covering the bead with pieces of stamped paper.

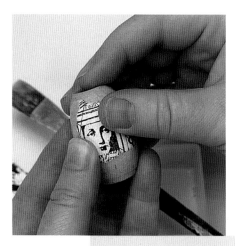

8] When the glue is dry, use the stipple brush to apply a straw color to various degrees. Remember to stamp a little color off of the brush onto scratch paper before applying it directly to the stamped image. This will avoid any big splotches of ink that are darker and more spotty than intended.

9] Use the colored pencils to color your images.

THIS *pretty bead started with black paper that was stamped and embossed in gold. The stamp is by JudiKins. After decoupaging the pieces of paper onto the bead, I used metallic pens to color it. I set the colors with a spray sealant and then applied two coats of the Crystal Cote glossy finish.*
➡➡

10] Thread the bead onto a skewer and spray it with a clear sealant. (If you don't, the stippled dye inks may run under the final gloss coat.)

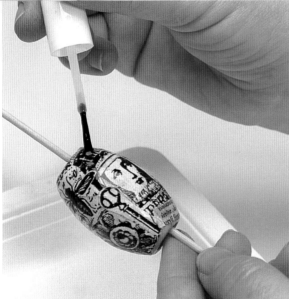

◀◀
ANOTHER *option is to paint the bead with acrylic paint, and then emboss it with a variety of colored embossing powders.*

11] Brush or spray a glossy finish onto your bead.

Shrink plastic basics

SHRINK PLASTIC IS SOMETHING YOU MAY RE-MEMBER FROM CHILD-HOOD, BUT I COULD SWEAR THAT THE NEW PRODUCTS GIVE MUCH MORE RELIABLE RE-SULTS. OK, MAYBE IT'S JUST ME, BUT TAKE AN-OTHER LOOK AT THIS PRODUCT. IT'S DOWN-RIGHT INSPIRATIONAL, WITH LOTS OF ROOM FOR EXPERIMENTATION. YOU CAN MAKE JEWELRY, DECORATIVE MEDAL-LIONS FOR BOOKS, HAIR ACCESSORIES AND FOR THE NEXT PROJECT, WE'LL MAKE OUR VERY OWN, VERY ORIGINAL PUSH PINS.

Shrinkage variation *

Shrink plastic shrinks a little shorter in one direction than in the other, so there may be a little distortion in your stamped images. That should be no problem.

The plastic shrinks 40 to 50 percent up, and the same amount inward, leaving you a piece of plastic that equals roughly one-half the size (both ways) of your original unbaked piece. If you want a piece of plastic that finish-es at 2" x 3" (5cm x 8cm), you must start with a piece that is about 4" x 6" (10cm x 15cm).

I usually bake my plastic at 225°F (107°C) for about five minutes or until shrinking stops. Don't preheat the oven—you want the plastic to slowly warm up. That will make it curl a lot less than with the high, ferocious heat of a gun.

Black shrink plastic *

The black shrink plastic melts faster and gooier than the others. When you stamp an image into the hot, black plastic for an in-taglio effect, you must wait for the shrink plastic to cool before taking the stamp off, or the plastic will stick to the stamp. Inking the stamp with clear embossing ink will keep it from sticking too much, but this is usually unnecessary.

Flat vs. intaglio *

When I'm doing an intaglio piece I use my heat gun and do one piece at a time. When I want a flat, stamped piece, I stamp and color all the images, cut them out and bake them on a Teflon-coated cookie sheet. After bak-ing, place a heavy acrylic block onto them to flatten them completely as they cool. They'll pop right off the cookie sheet after they have cooled down.

Mixed media *

The secret for getting your Metallic Rub-on or pigment ink colors to show more vibrantly on any of the plastics, but especially the black, is to first apply a light coat of silver Rub 'n Buff to the top layers of plastic. Don't put so much on your finger that it gets down into the imprinted image. If you do put too much silver ink on your plastic, use the sol-vent-based stamp cleaner to clean it off.

To get colored pencils, watercolor markers or chalk to stick to the unbaked plastic, first sand it lightly with fine-grit sandpaper. If you use a water-soluble product or chalks to color the plastic, seal the piece with an acrylic spray sealant such as Krylon Crystal Clear or Workable Krylon Fixatif for permanence.

Sanding the plastic first will also aid in getting a cleanly stamped impression. If you don't get a good impression with the ink, just wipe it off with cleaner and reapply.

Tap your project with embossing ink and sprinkle different powders on it for interesting textures. Stamp and emboss images right onto the plastic before and after shrinking.

Webbing spray on the unbaked product condenses into a nice texture when baked. Acrylic paint also bakes down to an interesting, nubby texture.

Try fusing scrap pieces of plastic together for a modern sculptural look. Weave them together and use a skewer to mold them to shape while they are hot.

If you've been working a piece and doing it over and over and hating every stamping or color combination, reheat it and squash it into an unusual shape or smash a stamp into the hot plastic for an intaglio look and recolor it. Fuse it onto another piece or drill a hole in it to make an unusual charm to dangle off your really funky-cool art. Just don't throw it away! There is never a reason to throw this product away.

Experiment heavily and happily with your shrink plastic. There is a whole realm of possibilities that haven't even been explored yet. You may just be the first one to come up with a new and fabulous technique!

←≡
THIS *book cover is stamped and embossed with a stamp from* STEPHANIE OLIN'S *rubber stamps. The center embellishment is a piece of black shrink art stamped with a Claudia Rose stamp in the intaglio method and finished with Metallic Rub-ons and a coat of Diamond Glaze.*

shrink art
push pins

I made lots of these push pins for Christmas gifts and everyone loved them. Then I started making them as small hostess gifts, so I started getting lots of orders and requests to make more. That's how I know your friends will love these adorable little packets too. Read on to learn how to produce shrink art treasures right down to the final packaging ready for gift giving or selling.

MATERIALS

SHINK ART PINS

* *black, clear and opaque shrink plastic*
* *two pieces of ¼" (6mm) foamcore cut to 2½" x 3½" (6cm x 9cm)*
  or
  one piece of ½" (12mm) thick foamcore cut to 2½" x 3½" (6cm x 9cm)
* *decorative paper to cover the foamcore*
* *six push pins*
* *product labels (I made the labels on my computer and printed them out in sheets with four labels on a sheet. Gifts always look more attractive if you include labels and present them in cool packaging.)*
* *piece of felt*
* *clear plastic wrap*

OTHER ART SUPPLIES

* *plastic plate and felt for your inkpad*
* *permanent ink for nonporous surfaces in colors of your choice*
* *permanent ink cleaner to clean your stamps and also to clean bad stampings and ugly colors off your plastic*
* *colored markers for nonporous surfaces*
* *Metallic Rub-ons*
* *silver Rub 'n Buff*
* *instant glue (I used QuickTite)*
* *tacky glue*
* *glaze (I use JudiKins' Diamond Glaze, Dimensional Magic and 3-D Crystal Lacquer)*
* *ultrafine sandpaper*

1] To make an intaglio piece, cut out a shape freehand. Remember to make it twice the size as you want the finished piece to be. Shrink it with your heat gun and impress a stamp into the hot plastic. Let the plastic cool a little before removing the stamp.

2] Dab a little silver Rub 'n Buff onto the raised image.

3] Use Metallic Rub-ons to give the image color. Lightly dab this product over the silver. While it's wet, it can accidentally be wiped right off very easily.

4] When the colors look just right, coat the piece with one of the glossy finishes and let it dry. I use Diamond Glaze, 3-D Crystal Lacquer or Dimensional Magic to get a nice, shiny, raised and rounded finish.

5] Cut a heart out of the clear plastic, sand lightly on both sides and use permanent markers to color the back side.

6] Heat it with the gun and stamp into it with the stamp. I used a swirl design by Christine Miller for Moe Wubba.

7] Put the silver and the colored rub-ons on the raised part of the image, letting the pretty basecoat colors show through.

8] Finish with Diamond Glaze.

9] Scratch both the push pin and the shrink art with your knife or an awl. Put a spot of instant glue on the pin and press both pieces together. Hold for about five seconds.

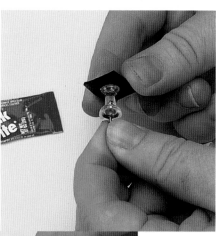

11] Wrap your set in clear plastic wrap, and you have the finished project!

10] To make the packaging, you can glue the two pieces of ¼" (6mm) foamcore together (or use ½" [12mm] foamcore) and then wrap it like it's a present. Sign the back of your set and glue the label on top.

more shrink art ideas

Dragonfly Dreams *

This little necklace would make an adorable and cherished gift for a special young lady. It is easy to make with lots of room for creativity. Imagine the fun that your pre-teen and her friends could have while spending an afternoon creating their own unique accessories. Remember to have a responsible person watching the oven. The dragonfly image is made with a stamp from Stephanie Olin's Rubber Stamps.

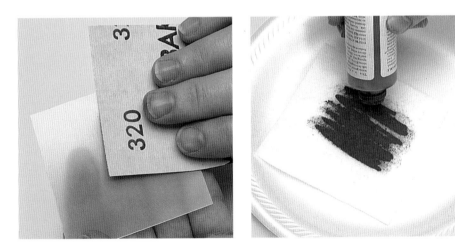

1] Use the opaque shrink plastic and sand it lightly.

2] Make an inkpad for yourself by placing a piece of felt on a plastic plate and inking it with permanent ink. I usually use black ink for this, but blue works just as well, since shrinking the plastic darkens the ink color.

3] Stamp your image. Remember, if you stamp a bad impression, wipe it off with permanent ink cleaner and start over.

4] Color the image with colored markers for nonporous surfaces. You can certainly substitute colored pencils, chalks or a number of other coloring implements.

 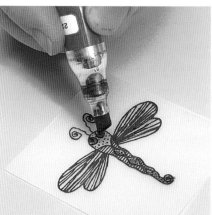

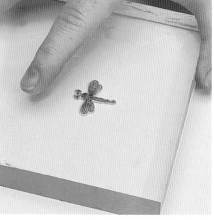 

5] Cut out the dragonfly, leaving about a 1/8" (3mm) margin. Use the 1/8" hole punch to make holes in the wings. (If you forget to punch holes before baking, you can drill them with a pin vise afterward.) Bake in an oven until they stop curling and shrinking, then take them out and put them under a large acrylic block so they will flatten as they cool.

6] Finish with a coat of Diamond Glaze or a similar product. Join the dragonflies with brass jump rings.

Firestorm *

This is a pin that was woven with scraps of shrink plastic, sprinkled with embossing powder and then shrunk with a heat gun. The little people are HO-scale train layout people that I painted with silver acrylic paint.

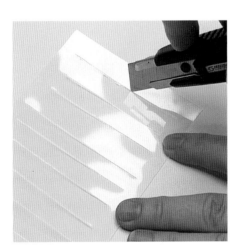

1] To make a woven pin, simply cut slits in a sheet of plastic and weave the scrap pieces into it after coloring it. Try stamping only bits and pieces of an image for an interesting texture.

2] Dab some embossing ink on the un-heated piece and lightly sprinkle some embossing powders onto it. Use the heat gun to heat and while still warm use a skewer to shape it a little. You can now glue trinkets onto it, drill holes and hang stuff on it to make a pin, add it to a larger sculpture ... and on and on.

gallery

◄ **THIS** *little lady started life as a cheap plastic fashion doll. After her haircut and makeover with Instant Iron and Instant Rust from Modern Options, she was treated to an ensemble made of stamped mulberry paper and plaster cloth.* THE STAMP IS FROM TOO MUCH FUN.

↑ **THIS** *is a large, wooden bead that has been painted with Instant Iron and then rusted with Instant Rust. It was then stamped and embossed with verdigris powder and trapped in a beaded wire.* THE STAMP USED IS MOE WUBBA.

PAPERCLAY PINS: *The hand stamp is from* ACEY DEUCY *and the swirl background is* RUBBER STAMPEDE. *Both pieces were basecoated with black acrylic paint and then topped with Metallic Rub-ons. The center pin uses a stamp from* GAINS & MCCALL *and is basecoated with gold acrylic paint and topcoated with black Metallic Rub-ons. The last pin was stamped with* CLEARSNAP *stamps, basecoated with green paint and topped with a wash of gold acrylic paint. The holes were drilled with a pin vise and the wire and beads were added last.*

➤ **THIS** *is a larger version of the mini oval purse, made with a heavier cord. It is designed to be worn slung across the body. The text stamp is from* TIN CAN MAIL *and the large and small African motif in the monoprinted paper are stamps from* JUDIKINS.

↑ A SELECTION *of paper clay beads.*
STAMPS ARE FROM JUDIKINS.

↑ THE *basic shape for this mini frame is cut from foam core. After the edges were spackled and dried, the entire frame was basecoated with gold acrylic paint, stamped and painted with a white wash and further embellished with odds and ends. The text stamp is from* TIN CAN MAIL *and the splatter stamp is from* DENAMI. *The woman in the photo is Lena Baker.*

↑ HERE'S *a mixed media piece with a paperclay face, stamped and embossed artwork, found objects and fabric paint.*
STAMPS USED ARE GAINS & MCCALL, STAMPINGTON & COMPANY AND MOE WUBBA.

◀◀ PATTERNED on the star book format, this little book is meant to be a sampler of stamped papers showing different techniques. The book front and back is covered with twist paper that has been flattened out and painted with dye inks and a gold Krylon marker. The center medallion on the front cover is a piece of Friendly Plastic (now distributed only by Stamp Oasis) that was stamped while still warm.
STAMP CREDITS: CLAUDIA ROSE, STEPHANIE OLIN'S RUBBER STAMPS, ACEY DEUCY, RUBBER MOON, DENAMI, ALL NIGHT MEDIA and STAMP FRANCISCO.

▶▶ THE medallion on the box top was a piece of chipboard colored black with a Sharpie and then tapped with different colors of pigment ink from Clearsnap. Three coats of Amazing Glaze were embossed onto the chipboard and then a stamp was impressed into the warm glaze. Beads were added after the Glaze was embossed onto the chipboard and then a stamp was impressed into the warm glaze. Beads were added after the glaze was cool and the entire piece was sealed with a coat of Diamond Glaze just to be sure the beads wouldn't fall off.
THE STAMP USED IS FROM JUDIKINS.

⬆ THE *Ducks in a Row stamp was embossed in copper powder on black paper. The center figure was foiled, with the black center being coated with Diamond Glaze and a sprinkling of glitter and tiny stars for depth. The swirls on the base paper are stamped with Tsukineko's Ultimate Metallic copper ink and the tiny stars and swirl stamps are from* JUDIKINS.

⬆ THIS *papier-maché box was painted with Instant Iron and rusted. The verdigris color was achieved by stamping a* POSH *splatter stamp all over inked with Tsukineko's Ultimate Metallic ink in teal.*

➥➤

THE *papier-maché box was painted with silver acrylic paint and tapped with Clearsnap's clear embossing powder. Silver powder was sprinkled on in an irregular pattern and embossed to achieve a rough look.*
The lid was cut out and replaced with a piece of clear styrene that was triple embossed wtih clear Amazing Glaze and then painted with a mixture of Diamond Glaze and colored dye re-inkers from Clearsnap and Tsukineko.

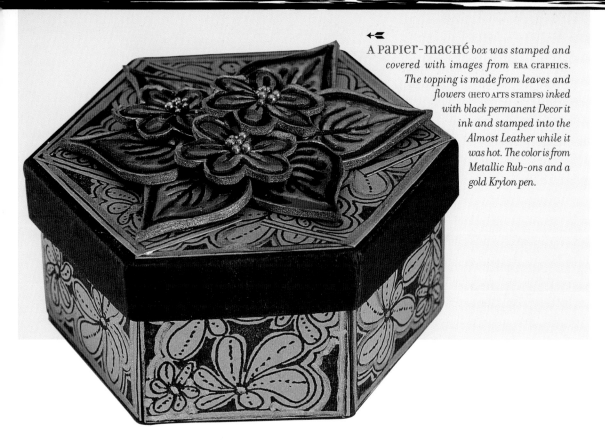

◄━ A papier-maché *box was stamped and covered with images from* ERA GRAPHICS. *The topping is made from leaves and flowers (*HERO ARTS STAMPS*) inked with black permanent Decor it ink and stamped into the Almost Leather while it was hot. The color is from Metallic Rub-ons and a gold Krylon pen.*

↑ THE *people pin is made with a base of thick chipboard, painted black and stamped. Then a layer of burned and poked copper is glued down with tacky glue. The people were made by stamping into a piece of brown Almost Leather with an uninked stamp from* ERA GRAPHICS. *The Almost Leather was rubbed with Metallic Rub-ons and highlighted with a gold Krylon pen. The sun pin is stamped into Almost Leather with a* STAMP OASIS *rubber stamp. After coloring, some areas were treated to a coat of Diamond Glaze.*

Resources

STAMPS *

Acey Deucy
P.O. Box 194
Ancram, NY 12502

American Art Stamp
3892 Del Amo Blvd.
Ste. 701
Torrance, CA 90503
www.americanartstamp.com

Claudia Rose
15 Baumgarten
Saugerties, NY 12477

**Creative Block/
Stampers Anonymous**
20613 Center Ridge Rd.
Rocky River, OH 44116
www.stampersanonymous.com

ERA Graphics
2476 Ottowa Way
San Jose, CA 95130
www.eragraphics.com

Hero Arts
1343 Powell St.
Emeryville, CA 94608
www.heroarts.com

Impress Me Rubber Stamps
17116 Escalon Drive
Encino, CA 91436-4030
impressme@earthlink.com

JudiKins
17803 S. Harvard Blvd.
Gardena, CA 90248
www.judi-kins.com

Magenta Rubber Stamps
351 Rue Blain
Mont Saint Hilaire
Quebec J3H 3B4
Canada
www.magentarubberstamps.com

Moe Wubba
(out of business)

Personal Stamp Exchange (PSX)
360 Sutton Pl.
Santa Rosa, CA 95407
www.psxstamps.com

Posh Impressions
22600-A Lambert St.
Ste. 706
Lake Forest, CA 92630
www.poshimpressions.com

Rubber Moon
P.O. Box 3258
Hayden Lake, ID 83835

Stamp Francisco
Coco Stamp
1248 Ninth Ave.
San Francisco, CA 94122

Stampington & Company
22992 Mill Creek Dr.
Ste. B
Laguna Hills, CA 92653
www.stampington.com

Stephanie Olin's Rubber Stamps
6171 Foxshield Dr.
Huntington Beach, CA 92647
http://home.flash.net/~olinstmp/

Tin Can Mail
c/o Stamp Rosa
60 Maxwell Court
Santa Rosa, CA 95401
(800) 554-5755
www.stamparosa.com

Toomuchfun
(out of business)

Zettiology
P.O. Box 2665
Renton, WA 98056

SUPPLIES *

Binney & Smith, Inc.
1100 Church Lane
Easton, PA 18044
www.binney-smith.com
distributors of Crayola and Liquitex products

Clearsnap, Inc.
Box 98
Anacortes, WA 98221
www.clearsnap.com
pens, inks, stamps and Penscore

Fiskars, Inc.
7811 W. Stewart Ave.
Wausau, WI 54401
www.fiskars.com
scissors and paper cutters

Marvy-Uchida
3535 Del Amo Blvd.
Torrance, California 90503
www.uchida.com
markers

Nasco Arts & Crafts
4825 Stoddard Rd.
Modesto, CA 95356
(800) 558-9595
e-mail: info@nascofa.com
Crayola brushes, Krylon sprays

Ranger Industries
15 Park Rd.
Tinton Falls, NJ 07724
www.rangerink.com

Rupert, Gibbon & Spider, inc.
P.O. Box 425
Healdsburg, CA 95448
(800) 442-0455
www.jacquardproducts.com
Methocel

Suze Weinberg Design Studio
39 Old Bridge Dr.
Howell, NJ 07731
www.schmoozewithsuze.com
Ultra Thick Embossing Enamel

Tsukineko
15411 N.E. Ninety-fifth St.
Redmond, WA 98052
www.tsukineko.com
pens and inks

US ArtQuest, Inc.
7800 Ann Arbor Rd.
Grass Lake, MI 49240
www.usartquest.com
Perfect Paper Adhesive

VIP
1215 N. Grove St.
Anaheim, CA 92806
foils and webbing spray

*Where I get my drawings and engravings
turned into rubber stamps*

Rand'M Engraving
15230 San Fernando Mission Blvd.
B101
Mission Hills, CA 91345
(818) 365-7557

index